My
First Book of

MANDARIN

FOR MY WIFE, ABBY, WHO
LOVES AND SUPPORTS ME
IN EVERYTHING. AND FOR
MY PARENTS, MEICHU AND
CHIENKUO, FOR ALL THAT
THEY HAVE TAUGHT ME.
—T.T.

BUSHEL
& PECK
BOOKS

Text copyright © 2023 by Timothy Tsai.

Published by Bushel & Peck Books, a family-run publishing house in Fresno, California,
that believes in uplifting children with the highest standards of art, music, literature, and
ideas. Find beautiful books for gifted young minds at www.bushelandpeckbooks.com.

Type set in Providence Sans, Learning Curve, Halewyn, and Chelsea Pro.
Artwork licensed from Shutterstock.com.

Bushel & Peck Books is dedicated to fighting illiteracy all over the world. For every
book we sell, we donate one to a child in need—book for book. To nominate a school or
organization to receive free books, please visit www.bushelandpeckbooks.com.

LCCN: 2022943082
ISBN: 9781638190462

First Edition

Printed in China

10 9 8 7 6 5 4 3 2 1

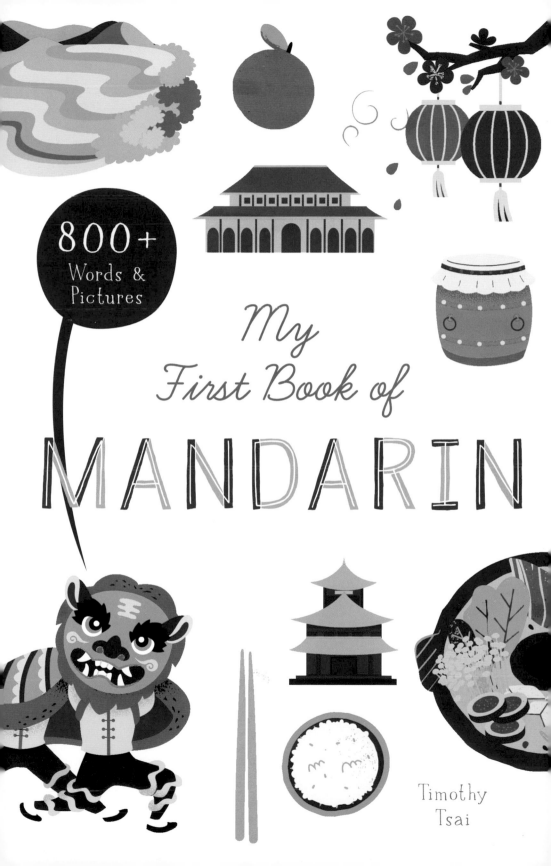

800+
Words &
Pictures

My
First Book of

MANDARIN

Timothy
Tsai

Contents

hello!
你好
nǐ hǎo

THE CHINESE
LANGUAGE
SYSTEM

About Mandarin

Hello and nǐ hǎo! Welcome to the start of your adventure in learning Mandarin Chinese.

In China, there are many dialects (versions) of Chinese. They all use the same Chinese characters, but each dialect pronounces those characters in different ways. Most of the dialects sound so different that it is almost impossible to understand a different dialect without learning and practicing it (for example, a person who speaks the Cantonese dialect would have no idea what a person speaking the Hakka dialect was saying). However, there is one dialect that is most common among Chinese speakers, and that is Mandarin! Mandarin Chinese is known as *Pǔtōnghuà* 普通话 (the "common language"). Almost everyone in China speaks Mandarin, including those who speak other dialects. So, to get around China, Mandarin is the place to start!

WHAT YOU'LL SEE IN THIS BOOK

Throughout the book, you will see Mandarin Chinese written in two different ways: Pinyin and simplified Chinese characters.

PINYIN

The first translation is what we call Pinyin (*pīnyīn* 拼音). Pinyin is the romanized version of Mandarin Chinese. It was first created in the 1950s by a man named Zhōu Yǒuguāng. He and his team spent over three years developing a system of learning Mandarin with the Latin alphabet so that the whole world could learn how to read and understand Chinese.

CHINESE CHARACTERS

The second translation you will see are the Chinese characters. There are two types of Chinese characters: traditional and simplified. Both types share many of the same characters, but the simplified version usually has characters that use fewer strokes than their traditional counterparts. Because simplified characters are the most widely used type in the Chinese-speaking world, we will use that version of Chinese characters in this book.

Chinese characters are different from English words. Each Chinese character represents a one-syllable word. Some Chinese characters can have multiple meanings. For example, the character 月 (yuè) can either mean "moon" or the particle word for months of the year. This makes context very important!

It is believed that Chinese characters came from pictographs. For example, the character 人 (rén, meaning "person") looks like it came from a drawing of a person. The character 月 (yuè, meaning "moon") resembles the curved shape of the moon. Today, however, the vast majority of Chinese characters consist of pictophonetic characters. This means that they are made up of radicals (these suggest the meaning of a character) and phonetic elements (these indicate original pronunciation, which

person
rén

月
moon
yuè

may or may not represent modern pronunciation). For example, if you have the character 妈 (*mā*, meaning "mom"), the left half of the character is the same as 女 (*nǚ*, meaning "female"), indicating the radical, or meaning, of a woman. The right half of the character is the same as 马 (*mǎ*, meaning "horse"), indicating the phonetic element that hints at the pronunciation. With over 50,000 characters to date, the combinations of radicals and phonetics are endless and can no longer be drawn out like pictures in the past. But don't let that number scare you! Even an educated Chinese person usually only knows about 8,000 characters. And what's even better is that you only need to know about 2,000–3,000 characters to be able to read books or newspapers and to pass tests.

2 How to Read Pinyin

While Pinyin uses the same letters as the Latin alphabet, they don't always sound the same as they do in English. It is important that the proper pronunciation of each letter/letter combination is understood in order to read whole Pinyin words properly. This book will explain the pronunciation sounds in the closest possible way using sounds from the English language.

PRONOUNCING VOWELS

VOWEL	SOUND	TIPS
a	*aah*	This sounds like when the doctor tells you to say "aah."
o	*o*	The vowel "o" is rarely seen as a syllable by itself. It's usually paired with initial consonants "b," "p," "m," and "f" (discussed in the next part) to make sounds like *bo, po, mo, fo*. When the "o" is paired with one of these initials, the sound then needs to be pronounced with a slight oo sound before the o sound (like the *wa* part in "war").
e	*uhh* + smile	To make this sound, make the *uhh* sound you make when trying to stall a sentence. But while you make that sound, spread your lips like when you're smiling. Another way is to make the singular o sound from the "o" vowel, and while you are making the o sound, spread your lips like a smile.
i	*ee*	This sounds like the double ee sound in "feet."
u	*oo*	This sounds like the double oo sound in "fool."
ü	*ee* + kissing face	This is a tough sound, but you can do it! Start by making the sound of ee (see above) while pursing your lips like you're giving a kiss. Then you've got the "ü" sound!

PRONOUNCING INITIAL CONSONANTS

Consonants are much easier, because most of them follow the same sounds they have in English—with some exceptions.

VOWEL	SOUND
b	This is similar to English but not voiced as much (like the sound of the "p" in "speak").
p	This is similar to English but with a strong puff of breath and also not voiced as much (like the sound of the "p" in "pork").
m	This is pronounced like it is in English.
f	This is pronounced like it is in English.
d	This is similar to English but not voiced as much (like the sound of the "t" in "stand").
t	This is similar to English but not voiced as much (like the sound of the "t" in "tea").
n	This is pronounced like it is in English.
l	This is pronounced like it is in English.
g	This is pronounced like it is in English.
k	This is pronounced like it is in English.
h	This is pronounced like it is in English.
w	This is pronounced like it is in English.
y	This is pronounced like it is in English.
j	This is similar to English but not voiced as much (like the sound of the "j" in "jeep").
q	This is pronounced *chee* (like the sound made when saying the "chee" in "cheese").
x	This is made by saying "she" while smiling. It's a tough sound to make, and in order to do it properly, you must raise the middle of your tongue toward the roof of the mouth but not all the way touching. Then, with your teeth close together, gently blow out air, making a slight hissing sound followed by the ee sound.

z	This is pronounced *ds* (like the sound made when saying the "ds" in "lids").
c	This is pronounced *ts* (like the sound made when saying the "ts" in "cats").
s	This is pronounced like it is in English.
zh	This sounds like *ds* (see "z" above) but while curling your tongue to roof of your mouth. It's similar to the first sound of "jerk," but not quite as voiced.
ch	This sounds like the *ch* made in English (like the "ch" in "chirp") but with the tongue curled to the roof of your mouth. Start by making the "ch" sound you normally would make in English, and then you curl your tongue back and up to the roof of your mouth while holding that sound.
sh	This sounds like the *sh* made in English (like the "sh" in "she") but with the tongue curled to the roof of your mouth. Start by making the "sh" sound, and then you curl your tongue back and up to the roof of your mouth while holding that sound.
r	This is similar to English, but with an emphasis of the tongue curled to the roof of the mouth (like the sound made toward the end of saying the letter "r").

 You can hear examples of each vowel and initial consonant by scanning this code. Find "Activity 1" and click the headphones to listen.

Tones

The tones in Mandarin are the most important part of the language to master, because depending on the tone you use, the word you are saying can mean something else entirely.

For example, if you were to pronounce *ma* with the first tone (*mā* 妈), it would mean "mother." But if you were to pronounce it with the third tone (*mǎ* 马), it would mean "horse." So it is very important to make sure you are using the proper tones when speaking and reading Mandarin.

THE TONES

There are four basic tones and a fifth neutral tone.

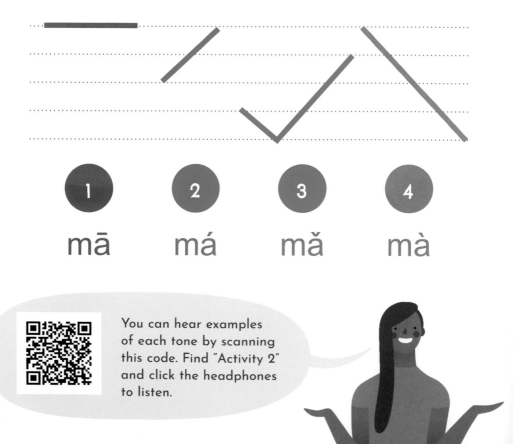

You can hear examples of each tone by scanning this code. Find "Activity 2" and click the headphones to listen.

TONE	MARKER	INTONATION
1 First tone	**—**	High pitch with an evenly prolonged sound, kind of like when the doctor tells you to say "aahh," but you are holding a higher pitch, evenly, for a longer period of time. Example: *mā* (妈) "mother/mom"
2 Second tone	**ˊ**	Medium pitch sliding to a high pitch, like when you are asking a question (what?). Whatever word you say with a second tone will sound like a question. Example: *má* (麻) "numb/numbness"
3 Third tone	**ˇ**	Medium-low pitch falling to a low pitch, then climbing up back to a medium-high pitch. It sounds similar to when you say "uh huh?" and your pitch drops and then climbs back up. Example: *mǎ* (马) "horse"
4 Fourth tone	**ˋ**	High pitch with a sharp and strong fall, much like when you say "No!" to someone. It is quick and sharp. Example: *mà* (骂) "scold/rebuke"
Neutral fifth tone	**No marker**	Medium pitch with a neutral and very short sound. It's like when you're saying a quick and urgent "but" when cutting into a sentence. Example: *ma* (吗) question particle

PRACTICING TONES

A helpful way to master tones is to move your hand in the direction of the tone when you are practicing words.

If you are saying *mā*, put your hand just above your head and draw out a flat line.

If you are saying *má*, put your hand just below your head and draw out a diagonal line that goes above your head.

If you are saying *mǎ*, put your hand just below your head and draw out a check mark that goes down to your chest and then back up to your head.

If you are saying *mà*, put your hand just above your head and draw out a diagonal line that falls sharply down to your chest.

TONE MARK PLACEMENT IN PINYIN

The tone marks are written above the main vowel of each syllable in a word. The main vowels follow this sequence/order:

a o e i u ü

So if you see "ao," like in *bào*, the main vowel is the "a." Or if you see "ie," like in *xiè*, the main vowel is the "e."

Note: There is one exception. Whenever the letters "i" and "u" are combined in a one-syllable word, like *iū* (*diū*) or *ui* (*dui*), the tone mark is then written on the second vowel.

ADDITIONAL TONE RULES

There are a few tonal rules that are important to remember when reading Mandarin. The reason for these extra rules is to make speaking easier and quicker with all the different tonal combinations in Mandarin.

1 If you ever see two third-tone words together, the first third-tone word will be pronounced with a second-tone sound.

Example: 你 *nǐ* (meaning "you") is a third-tone word. When you say the word by itself, it will be pronounced with the third-tone sound, which is a low-medium pitch dropping down to a low pitch and then climbing back up to a medium high pitch. But if you see the words 你好 *nǐ hǎo* (meaning "hello"), the *nǐ* part will be pronounced with the second tone and sound like *ní*, and the *hǎo* after will maintain the third tone. So on paper, you will see *nǐ hǎo*, but it will sound like *ní hǎo*.

2 If you ever have a third-tone word before a first-, second-, or fourth-tone word, you don't have to pronounce the third-tone word all the way through. For example, when we were learning how to say the third tone, we used the example of "uh-huh?" With this rule, you only need to sound out the "uh" part.

Example: If you see the words 考试 *kǎo shì* (meaning "exam" or "test"), the *kǎo* part is third tone and the *shì* part is fourth tone. If you said *kǎo* by itself, you would say it like a normal third tone by dropping the pitch from a medium-low to a low, and then bringing it back up to a medium-high pitch. But since it comes before a fourth-tone word, you will only drop it from a medium-low pitch to a low pitch. And then, you will move on to the second word, which is *shì*, and go from a high pitch to a sharp fall into a low pitch. Instead of resembling the "uh-huh?" we learned with the third tone, it will sound more like "uh-huh!"

3 If you ever see the number 一 *yī* (meaning "one") before a fourth-tone word, the *yī* is then pronounced with the second tone (*yí*).

Example: If you see the words 一下 *yī xià* (meaning "a moment" or "a bit"), the *yī* will change to a second-tone pronunciation because the *xià* following it is a fourth-tone word. So on paper, you will see *yī xià*, but it will sound like *yí xià*. Or if you see the words 一定 *yī dìng* (meaning "definitely" or "must"), the *yī* will change to a second tone because the *dìng* is fourth tone. So you will see *yī dìng* but you will pronounce it as *yídìng*.

4 If you ever see the number 一 *yī* (meaning "one") before a first-, second-, or third-tone word, the *yī* is then pronounced with the fourth tone (*yì*).

Example: If you see the words 一般 *yī bān* (meaning "generally" or "usually"), the *yī* will change to a fourth-tone pronunciation because the *bān* following it is a first-tone word. So on paper, you will see *yī bān*, but it will sound like *yì bān*. Or if you see the words 一起 *yī qǐ* (meaning "together"), the *yī* will change to fourth tone because the *qǐ* is third tone. So you will see *yī qǐ*, but you will pronounce it as *yì qǐ*.

When you are counting numbers or items, the number 一 *yī* (meaning "one") alone stays the same. 十一 *shíyī* (meaning "eleven") also stays the same. But if you are saying "one hundred" (一百 *yī bǎi*), then the *yī* pronunciation changes to fourth tone (*yì*) because the *bǎi* after it is third tone. So you will see *yī bǎi*, but you will say *yì bǎi*.

> **Note: Rules 3 and 4 only apply to the number one (*yī* 一), so make sure you are cross-referencing the Chinese characters with the Pinyin. You don't want to accidentally pronounce a word like 医院 *yī yuàn* (meaning "hospital") into *yí yuàn* (which means "the final wishes of the departed")!**

5 If you ever see the word 不 *bù* (meaning "no" or "not") before a fourth-tone word, the *bù* is then pronounced with the second tone (*bú*).

> **Example: If you see the words 不是 *bù shì* (meaning "not it" or "to not be"), the *bù* will change to a second-tone pronunciation because the *shì* after it is a fourth-tone word. So on paper you will see *bù shì*, but it will sound like *bú shì*.**

It might sound like a lot, but don't worry! You'll eventually get the hang of it. With practice, the tones and their rules will become second nature to you.

And that about covers it! Now on to the vocabulary.

Look for the following tools to help you get the most out of this section:

 Example sentences: See vocabulary in context!

 Language tips: Get extra insight about the meaning or usage of certain words.

 Culture cues: Learn to love the Chinese culture alongside the language!

VOCABULARY

4

Greetings

good morning

早上好

zǎoshàng hǎo

hello

你好

nǐ hǎo

hello (formal)

您好

nín hǎo

good evening

晚上好

wǎnshàng hǎo

good night

晚安

wǎn ān

good afternoon

下午好

xiàwǔ hǎo

● Nice to meet you. I'm Wang He.

很高兴认识你. 我叫王河.

Hěn gāoxìng rèn shì nǐ. Wǒ Jiào Wáng Hé.

I look forward to working with you.

我期待和您一起合作.

Wǒ qídài hé nín yīqǐ hézuò.

bye / see you later

再见

zàijiàn

I am _____

我叫_____

Wǒ Jiào_____

💡 In Chinese culture, the family name holds the most importance, so when introducing oneself, the family (last) name comes before the person's given (first) name. For example, when saying my full name in English, I will normally say, "My name is Timothy (first name) Tsai (last name)." But when saying my full name in Chinese, it will be reversed, so I will say, "My name is Tsai Timothy."

23

Courtesy

please
请
qǐng

thank you
谢谢你
xièxiè nǐ

thank you very much
非常感谢
fēicháng gǎnxiè

you're welcome
别客气
bié kèqì

sorry
对不起
duìbùqǐ

excuse me
不好意思
bù hǎo yìsi

Really? Is that so?
真的吗？
Zhēn de ma?

that's right
是的
shì de

no
不
bù

yes
是
shì

25

People

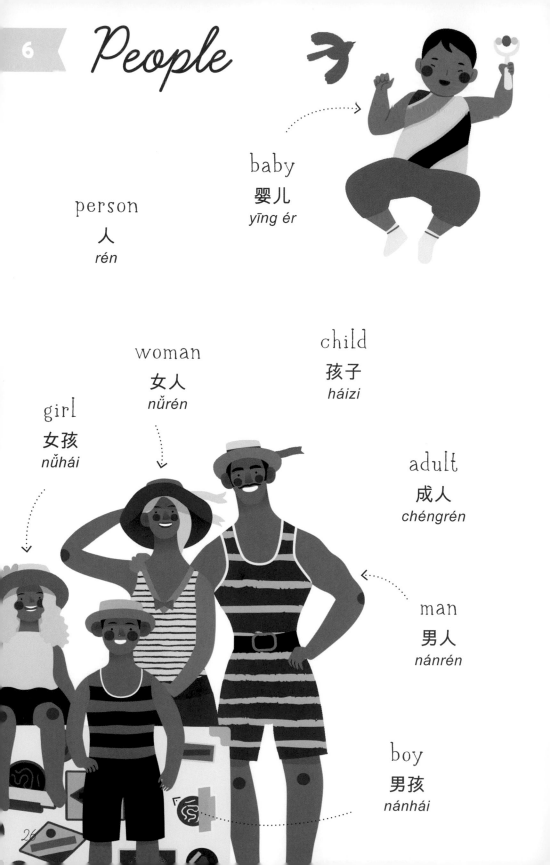

baby
婴儿
yīng ér

person
人
rén

child
孩子
háizi

woman
女人
nǚrén

girl
女孩
nǚhái

adult
成人
chéngrén

man
男人
nánrén

boy
男孩
nánhái

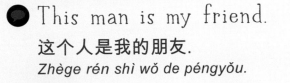

This man is my friend.
这个人是我的朋友.
Zhège rén shì wǒ de péngyǒu.

people
人们
rénmen

male
男性
nánxìng

female
女性
nǚxìng

friendly /
gentle
友善
yǒushàn

friend
朋友
péngyǒu

7

Personal Pronouns

HELLO
MY NAME IS

小明

name
名字
míngzi

Mr.
先生
Xiānshēng

Mrs.
太太
Tàitai

Ms. / Miss
小姐
Xiǎojiě

💡 This is also often used as a younger "Mrs." for politeness (Chinese people do not like to feel aged).

I / me
我
wǒ

my / mine
我的
wǒ de

you
你
nǐ

your
你的
nǐ de

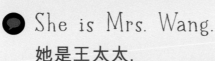

💬 She is Mrs. Wang.
她是王太太.
Tā shì Wáng tàitai.

💡 Notice that "she" and "he" are pronounced the same exact way, but the characters are different so that one can tell if it is a female or a male being discussed when reading.

we / us
我们
wǒmen

our
我们的
wǒmen de

everybody
大家
dàjiā

they / them
他们
tāmen

their
他们的
tāmen de

he his
他 他的
tā *tā de*

she her
她 她的
tā *tā de*

8

Water

ocean
海洋
hǎiyáng

water
水
shuǐ

waterfall
瀑布
pùbù

beach
海边
hǎibiān

sand
沙子
shāzi

sea
海
hǎi

shore
海滩
hǎitān

lake
湖
hú

river
河
hé

The Yellow River likely gets its name from the color of its muddy water.

Yellow River

黄河

huánghé

Yangtze River

长江

Chángjiāng

 The Yangtze River is the third-longest river in the world. The name literally translates to "Long River."

Pearl River

珠江

Zhūjiāng

Chinese junk

艚

cáo

 The junk was a wooden sailing ship used on both rivers and oceans for hundreds of years.

9

Land

land
土地
tǔdì

mountain
山
shān

the world
世界
shìjiè

Notice how the Chinese character looks like a mountain with three peaks!

region / area
地区
dìqū

geography
地理
dìlǐ

scenery / landscape
风景
fēngjǐng

plains
平原
píngyuán

💬 I climbed a mountain yesterday.
我昨天去爬山了.
Wǒ zuótiān qù páshānle.

hill
小山
xiǎoshān

slope /
incline
斜坡
xiépō

rock /
stone
石头
shítou

boulder
巨石
jùshí

Earth
地球
dìqiú

soil / dirt
土
tǔ

SOIL

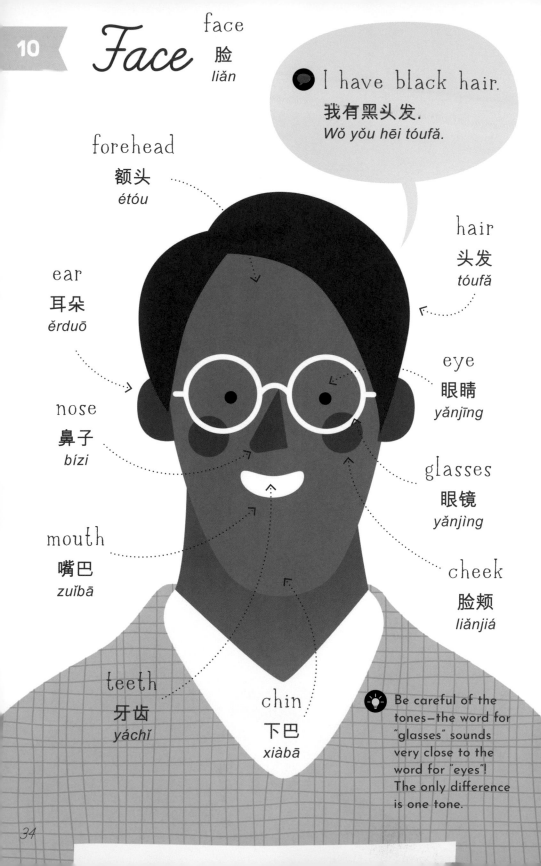

Face

face
脸
liăn

I have black hair.
我有黑头发.
Wŏ yŏu hēi tóufă.

forehead
额头
étóu

hair
头发
tóufă

ear
耳朵
ěrduō

eye
眼睛
yănjīng

nose
鼻子
bízi

glasses
眼镜
yănjing

mouth
嘴巴
zuĭbā

cheek
脸颊
liănjiá

teeth
牙齿
yáchĭ

chin
下巴
xiàbā

Be careful of the tones—the word for "glasses" sounds very close to the word for "eyes"! The only difference is one tone.

Body

body
身体
shēntǐ

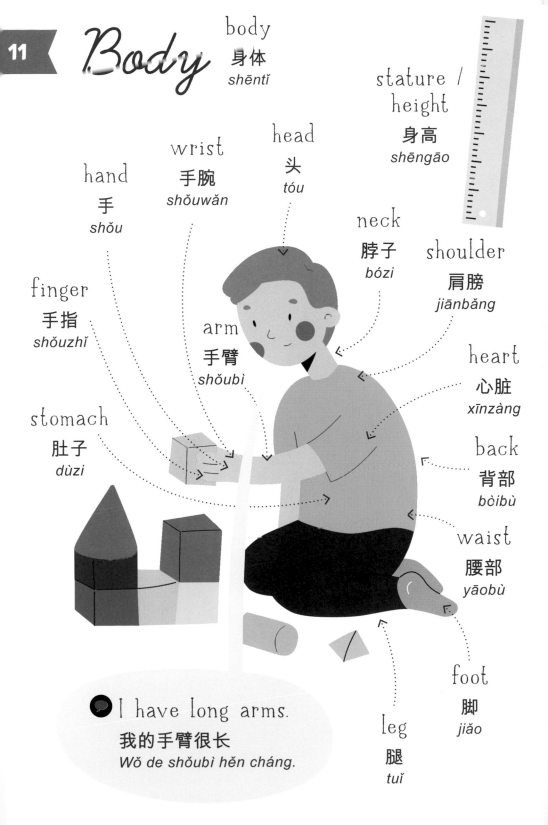

stature /
height
身高
shēngāo

wrist
手腕
shǒuwǎn

head
头
tóu

hand
手
shǒu

neck
脖子
bózi

shoulder
肩膀
jiānbǎng

finger
手指
shǒuzhǐ

arm
手臂
shǒubì

heart
心脏
xīnzàng

stomach
肚子
dùzi

back
背部
bèibù

waist
腰部
yāobù

foot
脚
jiǎo

leg
腿
tuǐ

I have long arms.
我的手臂很长
Wǒ de shǒubì hěn cháng.

Clothing

clothing
衣服
yīfú

to wear
穿
chuān

Tang suit
唐装
tángzhuāng

qipao
旗袍
qípáo

to take off
脱
tuō

💬 Your new qipao is beautiful!
你的新旗袍很漂亮!
Nǐ de xīn qípáo hěn piàoliang!

The Tang suit is a type of traditional Chinese jacket. It was commonly worn in the past, but today it's used for more formal occasions, such as celebrating Chinese New Year or weddings.

The qipao is the most famous traditional Chinese dress. Different regions have different styles.

trousers /
pants
裤子
kùzi

coat
外套
wàitào

hat / cap /
headwear
帽子
màozi

jacket
夹克
jiákè

shoe
鞋子
xiézi

shirt
衬衫
chènshān

T-shirt / tee shirt
T 恤
T xù

underclothing /
underwear
内衣
nèiyī

sock
袜子
wàzi

dress
裙子
qúnzi

skirt
短裙
duǎn qún

13

Colors

color
颜色
yánsè

suffix for color
色
sè

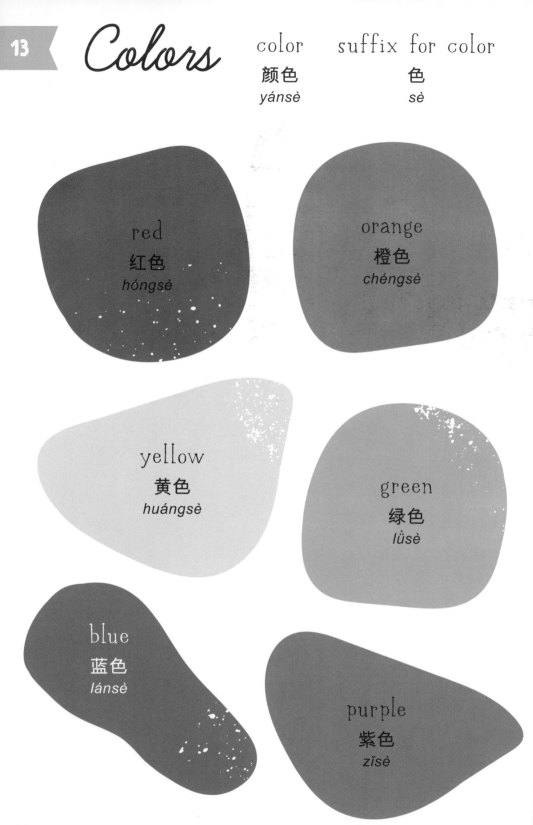

red
红色
hóngsè

orange
橙色
chéngsè

yellow
黄色
huángsè

green
绿色
lǜsè

blue
蓝色
lánsè

purple
紫色
zǐsè

My car is yellow.

我的车是黄色的.

Wǒ de chē shì huáng sè de.

white

白色

báisè

black

黑色

hēisè

gray

灰色

huīsè

gold

金色

jīnsè

silver

银色

yínsè

brown

咖啡色

kāfēisè

pink

粉色

fěnsè

Opposites

small
小
xiăo

big
大
dà

heavy
重
zhòng

light
轻
qīng

hot
热
rè

cold
冷
lěng

tall
高
gāo

short
矮
ǎi

full
满
mǎn

empty
空
kōng

dirty
脏
zāng

clean
干净
gānjìng

My Family

marriage
婚姻
hūnyīn

wedding
婚礼
hūnlǐ

to get
married
结婚
jiéhūn

parents
父母
fùmǔ

mom
妈妈
māma

dad
爸爸
bàba

son
儿子
érzi

YOU

daughter
女儿
nǚ ér

family
家庭
jiātíng

🔴 I love my family!
我爱我的家庭!
Wǒ ài wǒ de jiātíng!

sisters
姐妹
jiěmèi

brothers
兄弟
xiōngdì

older
sister
姐姐
jiějie

younger
sister
妹妹
mèimei

older
brother
哥哥
gēge

younger
brother
弟弟
dìdi

Father's Side

In Chinese, almost every member of the extended family has individual titles (more simple on the mom's side). While it becomes very complicated to learn, it allows for people to understand exactly who is being talked about.

grandpa	爷爷	yéye
grandma	奶奶	nǎinai
older uncle	伯伯	bóbo
older uncle's wife	伯母	bómǔ
younger uncle	叔叔	shūshu
younger uncle's wife	婶婶	shěnshen
older aunt	姑妈	gūmā
aunt's husband (both older and younger aunts)	姑父	gūfu
younger aunt	姑姑	gūgū
older cousin (uncle's boy)	堂哥	táng gē
younger cousin (uncle's boy)	堂弟	táng dì
older cousin (uncle's girl)	堂姐	táng jiě
younger cousin (uncle's girl)	堂妹	táng mèi
older cousin (aunt's boy)	姑表哥	gū biǎogē
younger cousin (aunt's boy)	姑表弟	gū biǎodì
older cousin (aunt's girl)	姑表姐	gū biǎojiě
younger cousin (aunt's girl)	姑表妹	gū biǎomèi

Mother's Side

grandpa	外公	*wàigōng*
grandma	外婆	*wàipó*
uncle (both older and younger)	舅舅	*jiùjiu*
uncle's wife (both older and younger uncles)	舅妈	*jiùmā*
older aunt	姨妈	*yímā*
younger aunt	阿姨	*āyí*
aunt's husband (both older and younger aunts)	姨父	*yífu*
older cousin (uncle or aunt's boy)	表哥	*biǎo gē*
younger cousin (uncle or aunt's boy)	表弟	*biǎo dì*
older cousin (uncle or aunt's girl)	表姐	*biǎojiě*
younger cousin (uncle or aunt's girl)	表妹	*biǎomèi*

💡 Even though the children of aunts from your father's side have a *gū* 姑 leading each title, they are still commonly referred to as only *biǎogē*, *biǎojiě*, *biǎodì*, or *biǎomèi* because it's easier to not have to say so many words!

Directions

directions
方向
fāngxiàng

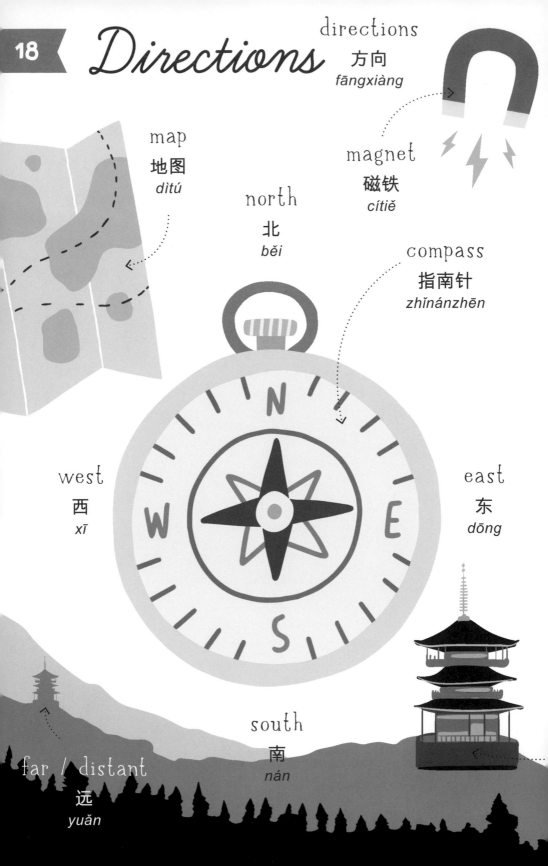

map
地图
dìtú

magnet
磁铁
cítiě

north
北
běi

compass
指南针
zhǐnánzhēn

west
西
xī

east
东
dōng

south
南
nán

far / distant
远
yuǎn

We need to go straight.
我们需要直走.
Wǒmen xūyào zhí zǒu.

up / above
上
shàng

down / under
下
xià

left
左
zuǒ

right
右
yòu

straight
直
zhí

near / close
靠近
kàojìn

19

Space

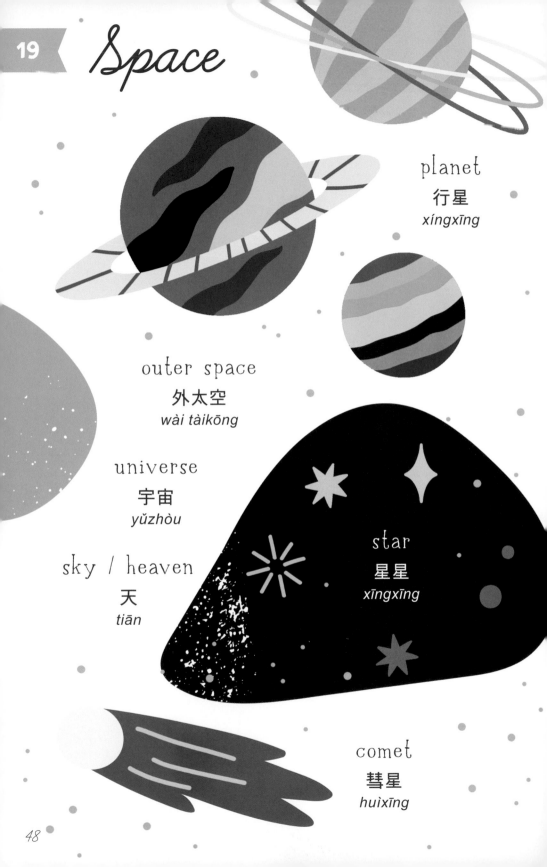

planet
行星
xíngxīng

outer space
外太空
wài tàikōng

universe
宇宙
yǔzhòu

sky / heaven
天
tiān

star
星星
xīngxīng

comet
彗星
huìxīng

I can see the stars in outer space.

我看的到外太空的星星.

Wǒ kàn de dào wài tàikōng de xīngxīng.

day
白天
báitiān

sun
太阳
tàiyáng

air
空气
kōngqì

sky
天空
tiānkōng

moon
月亮
yuèliàng

full moon
满月
mǎnyuè

Weather

weather
天气
tiānqì

clear
weather
晴天
qíngtiān

cloud
云
yún

thunder
雷
léi

storm
风暴
fēngbào

snow
雪
xuě

lightning
闪电
shǎndiàn

hail
冰雹
bīngbào

typhoon
台风
táifēng

tornado
龙卷风
lóngjuǎnfēng

rainbow
彩虹
cǎihóng

rain
雨
yǔ

wind
风
fēng

Plants

tree
树
shù

bamboo
竹子
zhúzi

woods /
grove
树林
shùlín

plant
植物
zhíwù

grass
草
cǎo

forest
森林
sēnlín

bush
灌木
guànmù

chrysanthemum
菊花
júhuā

peony
牡丹
mǔdān

leaf
叶子
yèzi

flower
花
huā

orchid
兰花
lánhuā

plum
blossom
梅花
méihuā

rose
玫瑰
méiguī

lotus flower
莲花 / 荷花
liánhuā / héhuā

Animals

animal
动物
dòngwù

cow
牛
niú

cat
猫
māo

whale
鲸鱼
jīngyú

sea
urchin
海胆
hǎidǎn

deer
鹿
lù

crab
螃蟹
pángxiè

fox
狐狸
húlí

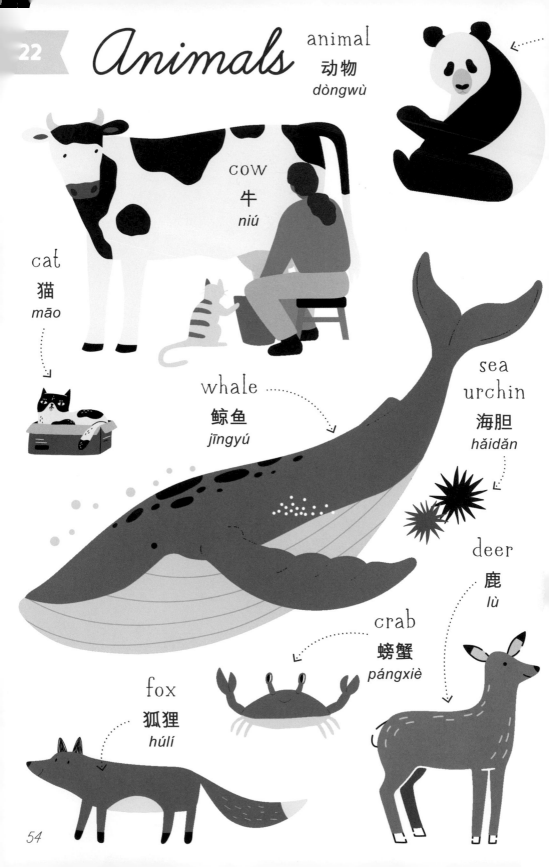

panda
熊猫
xióngmāo

sea turtle
海龟
hǎiguī

bear
熊
xióng

polar bear
北极熊
běijíxióng

starfish
海星
hǎixīng

bird
鸟
niǎo

lion
狮子
shīzi

elephant
大象
dà xiàng

sparrow
麻雀
máquè

crane
鹤
hè

chicken
鸡
jī

crow
乌鸦
wūyā

insect
昆虫
kūnchóng

butterfly
蝴蝶
húdié

moth
蛾
é

frog
青蛙
qīngwā

fish
鱼
yú

salmon
三文鱼
sānwényú

goldfish
金鱼
jīnyú

tuna
金枪鱼
jīnqiāngyú

flamingo
火烈鸟
huǒ liè niǎo

turtle
乌龟
wūguī

57

Chinese Zodiac

rat
鼠
shǔ

1948, 1960, 1972, 1984, 1996, 2008, 2020

ox
牛
niú

1952, 1964, 1976, 1988, 2000, 2012, 2024

snake
蛇
shé

1953, 1965, 1977, 1989, 2001, 2013, 2025

dragon
龙
lóng

monkey
猴子
hóuzi

1956, 1968, 1980, 1992, 2004, 2016, 2028

1957, 1969, 1981, 1993, 2005, 2017, 2029

rooster
公鸡
gōngjī

tiger
老虎
lǎohǔ

1950, 1962, 1974, 1986, 1998, 2010, 2022

1951, 1963, 1975, 1987, 1999, 2011, 2023

rabbit
兔子
tùzǐ

1955, 1967, 1979, 1991, 2003, 2015, 2027

horse
马
mǎ

1954, 1966, 1978, 1990, 2002, 2014, 2026

goat
羊
yáng

According to myth, the Jade Emperor (the ruler of heaven) wanted a way of measuring time, with twelve hours in each half of the day, twelve months in a year, and so on. He told all the animals that there would be a race and that each year of the zodiac would be named after the first twelve winners. The zodiac cycle (rat, ox, tiger, etc.) is in order of the winners! A person's Chinese zodiac animal depends on the year he or she was born.

1958, 1970, 1982, 1994, 2006, 2018, 2030

dog
狗
gǒu

pig
猪
zhū

1959, 1971, 1983, 1995, 2007, 2019, 2031

59

24

Seasons

the four seasons
四季
sì jì

season
季节
jìjié

Spring
春天
chūntiān

Summer
夏天
xiàtiān

Autumn / Fall
秋天
qiūtiān

Winter
冬天
dōngtiān

● Autumn is the best season.
秋天是最好的季节.
Qiūtiān shì zuì hǎo de jìjié.

year
年
nián

this year
今年
jīnnián

last year
去年
qùnián

next year
明年
míngnián

every year
每年
měinián

Months

month
月
yuè

💡 Notice that the names of each month are the numbers one to twelve followed by the word for "month."

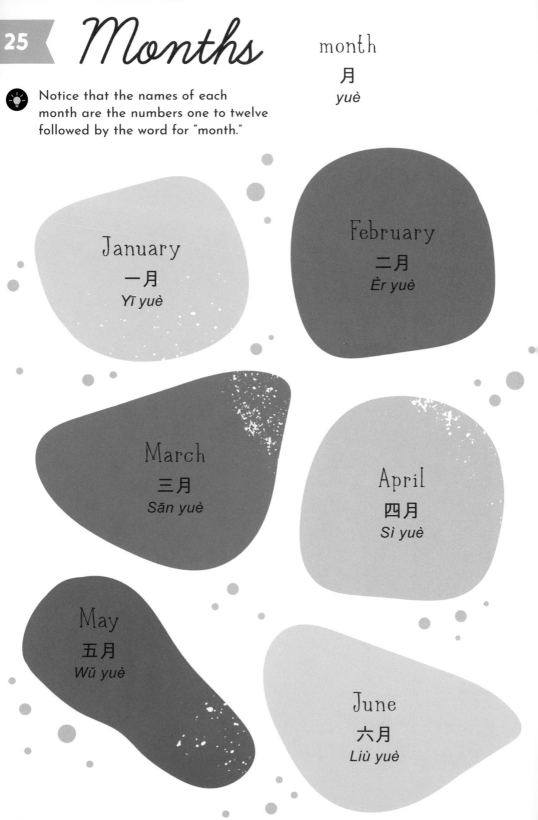

January
一月
Yī yuè

February
二月
Èr yuè

March
三月
Sān yuè

April
四月
Sì yuè

May
五月
Wǔ yuè

June
六月
Liù yuè

this
month
这个月
zhège yuè

next
month
下个月
xià gè yuè

last
month
上个月
shàng gè yuè

every
month
每个月
měi gè yuè

July
七月
Qī yuè

August
八月
Bā yuè

September
九月
Jiǔ yuè

October
十月
Shí yuè

November
十一月
Shíyī yuè

December
十二月
Shí èr yuè

26

Days of the Week

calendar
日历
rìlì

week
星期 / 周
xīngqí / zhōu

weekday / workday
工作日
gōngzuò rì

this week
这个星期
zhège xīngqí

next week
下个星期
xià gè xīngqí

last week
上个星期
shàng gè xīngqí

💡 In Chinese, the way to name the days of the week is by saying the word for "week" (*xīngqí* 星期) followed by the counter of the day. For example, Monday is 1 (*yī* 一), Tuesday is 2 (*èr* 二), Wednesday is 3 (*sān* 三), and so forth until Sunday, which is instead defined by 日 *rì*.

💡 Notice that Sunday is the only day that is not counted by a number. Interestingly, the 日 *rì* character is the character used for the word "sun."

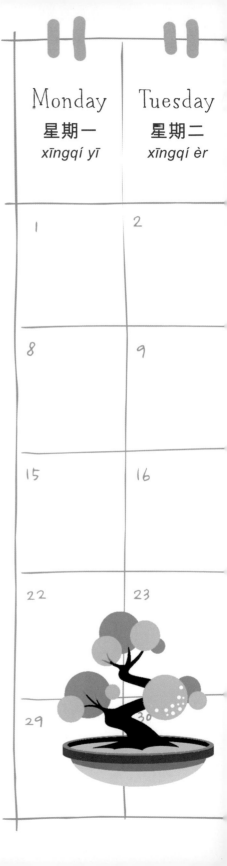

Monday 星期一 *xīngqí yī*	Tuesday 星期二 *xīngqí èr*
1	2
8	9
15	16
22	23
29	30

27

Time

十一点
shíyī diǎn

time
时间
shíjiān

十点
shí diǎn

watch
手表
shǒubiǎo

九点
jiǔ diǎn

morning / AM
上午
shàngwǔ

八点
bā diǎn

afternoon / PM
下午
xiàwǔ

七点
qī diǎn

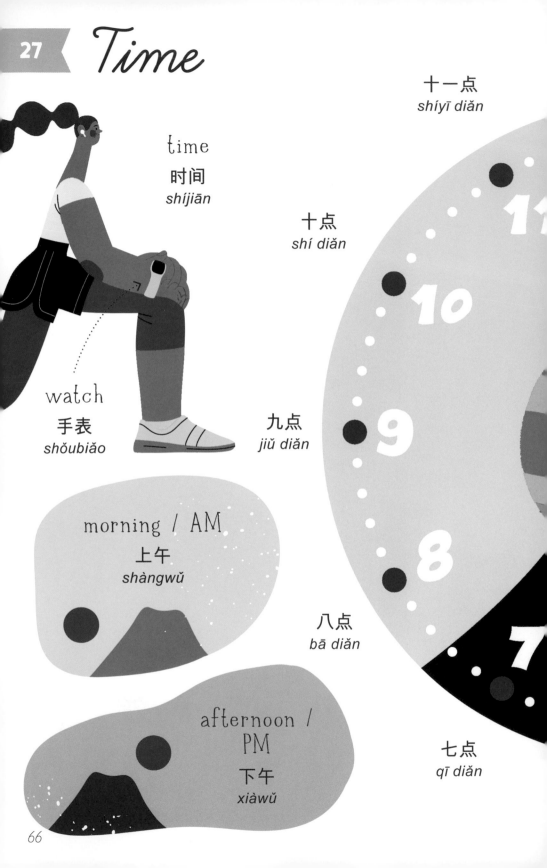

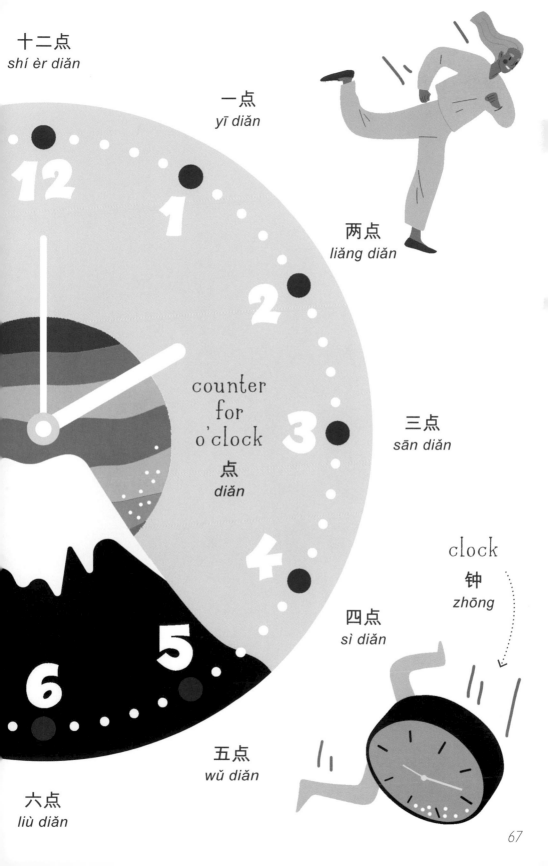

十二点
shí èr diǎn

一点
yī diǎn

两点
liǎng diǎn

counter
for
o'clock
点
diǎn

三点
sān diǎn

clock
钟
zhōng

四点
sì diǎn

五点
wǔ diǎn

六点
liù diǎn

28

Time of Day

now
现在
xiànzài

morning
早上
zǎoshàng

noon / midday
中午
zhōngwǔ

evening
傍晚
bāngwǎn

night
晚上
wǎnshàng

midnight
半夜
bànyè

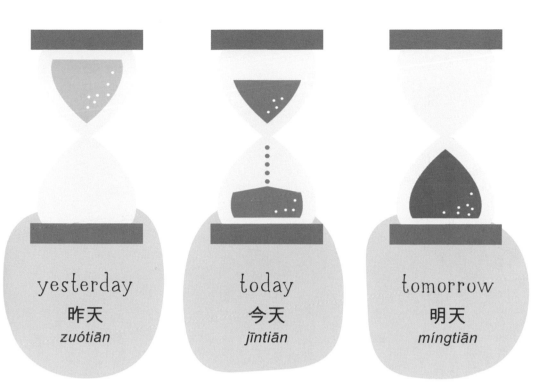

yesterday
昨天
zuótiān

today
今天
jīntiān

tomorrow
明天
míngtiān

every day
每天
měitiān

every night
每天晚上
měitiān wǎnshàng

every morning
每天早上
měitiān zǎoshàng

early
早
zǎo

late
晚
wǎn

sometimes
有时候
yǒu shíhòu

When?
什么时候
Shénme shíhòu

What time?
几点
Jǐ diǎn

69

29

Countries

country
国家
guójiā

president
总统
zǒngtǒng

government
政府
zhèngfǔ

China
中国
Zhōngguó

America /
United States
美国
Měiguó

Chinese
person
中国人
Zhōngguó rén

American
person
美国人
Měiguó rén

suffix indicating a person
is from a given country
人
rén

Ūrūmqi

Xinjiang

Tibet

Lhasa

population
人口
rénkǒu

prefecture /
state
州
zhōu

county
县
xiàn

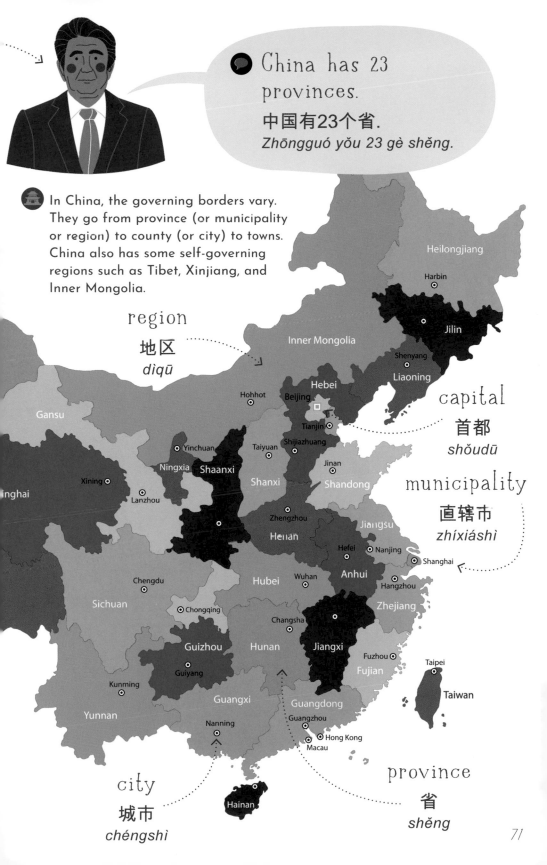

China has 23 provinces.

中国有23个省.

Zhōngguó yǒu 23 gè shěng.

In China, the governing borders vary. They go from province (or municipality or region) to county (or city) to towns. China also has some self-governing regions such as Tibet, Xinjiang, and Inner Mongolia.

region

地区

dìqū

capital

首都

shǒudū

municipality

直辖市

zhíxiáshì

city

城市

chéngshì

province

省

shěng

30

Urban and Rural

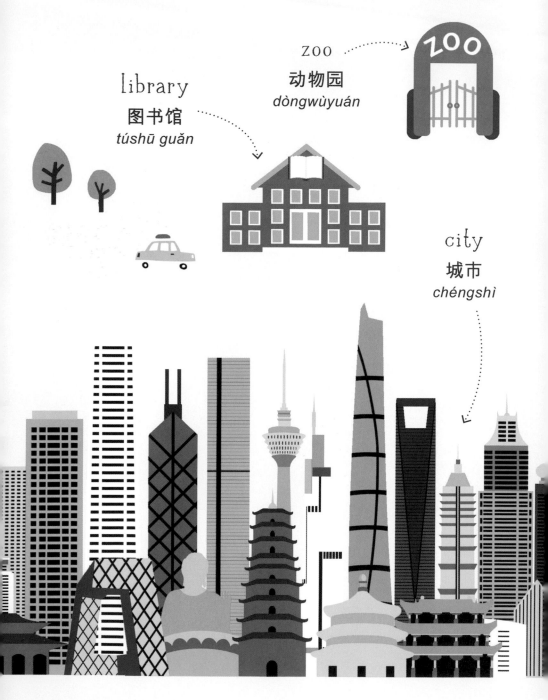

zoo
动物园
dòngwùyuán

library
图书馆
túshū guǎn

city
城市
chéngshì

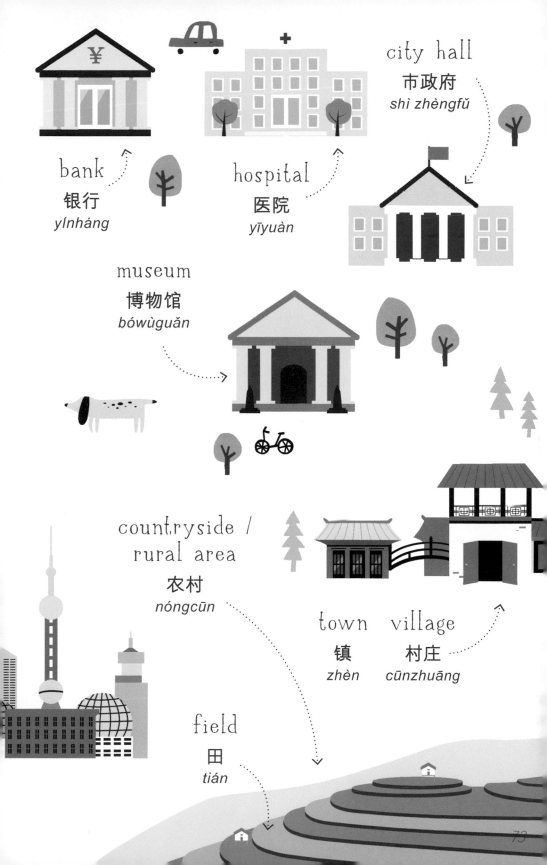

bank
银行
yínháng

hospital
医院
yīyuàn

city hall
市政府
shì zhèngfǔ

museum
博物馆
bówùguǎn

countryside / rural area
农村
nóngcūn

town
镇
zhèn

village
村庄
cūnzhuāng

field
田
tián

31

Transportation

to go
去
qù

transportation
运输
yùnshū

EXPRESS

traffic jam
堵车
dǔchē

bus stop
公交车站
gōngjiāo chēzhàn

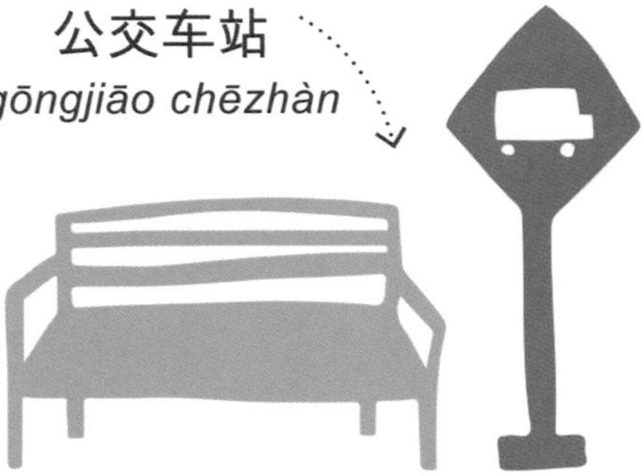

street
街道
jiēdào

traffic light
红绿灯
hónglǜdēng

bus
公交车
gōngjiāo chē

to come
来
lái

taxi
出租车
chūzū chē

car
车
chē

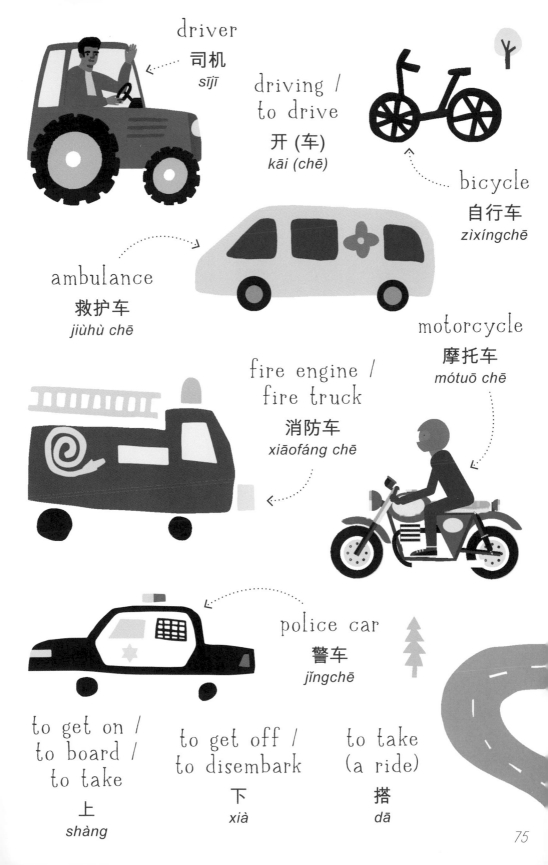

driver
司机
sījī

driving /
to drive
开 (车)
kāi (chē)

bicycle
自行车
zìxíngchē

ambulance
救护车
jiùhù chē

motorcycle
摩托车
mótuō chē

fire engine /
fire truck
消防车
xiāofáng chē

police car
警车
jǐngchē

to get on /
to board /
to take
上
shàng

to get off /
to disembark
下
xià

to take
(a ride)
搭
dā

75

Some Chinese bullet trains can travel up to 373 miles (600 km) per hour!

bullet train
高铁
gāotiě

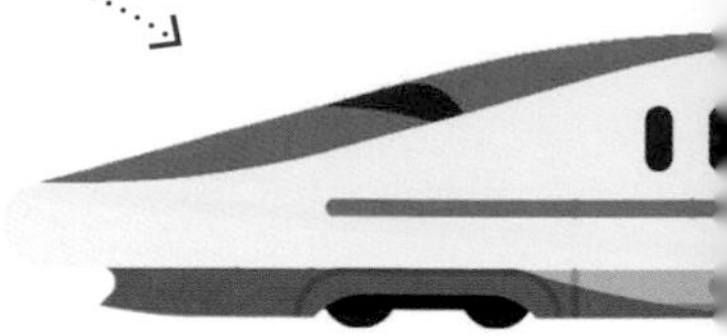

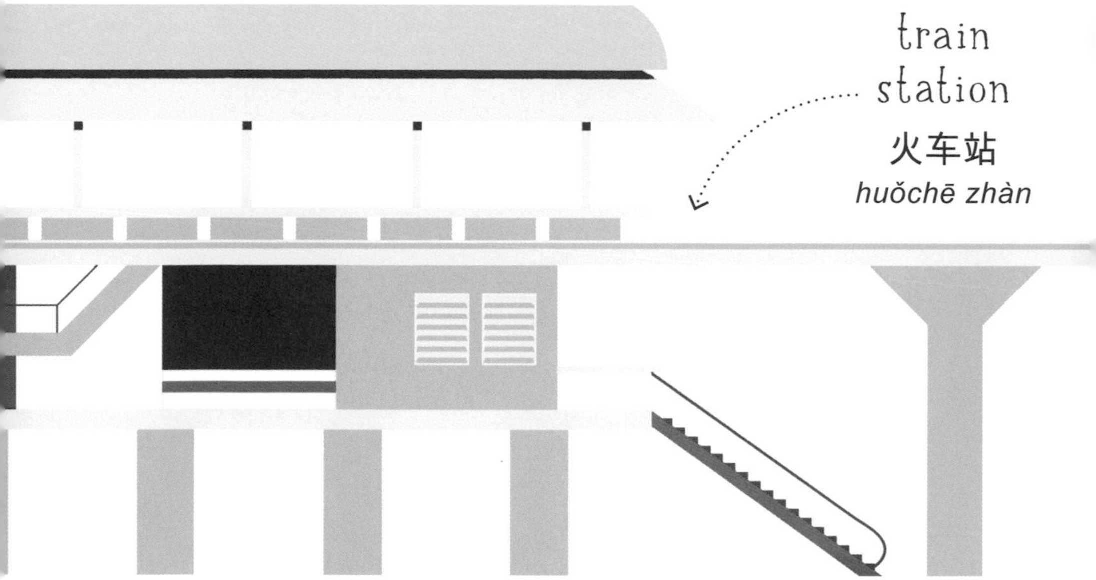

train station
火车站
huǒchē zhàn

train
火车
huǒchē

subway
地铁
dìtiě

ticket
票
piào

airplane

飞机

fēijī

airport

飞机场

fēijī chǎng

to fly

飞

fēi

boat

船

chuán

harbor

港口

gǎngkǒu

32

Travel

tourism
旅游
lǚyóu

to travel / trip / journey
旅行
lǚxíng

sightseeing
观光
guānguāng

inn
旅馆
lǚguǎn

hotel
酒店
jiǔdiàn

vacation
假期
jiàqī

travel agency
旅行社
lǚxíngshè

reservation
预订
yùdìng

overseas travel
海外旅游
hǎiwài lǚyóu

passport
护照
hùzhào

PASSPORT

💬 I'm going to travel for one year.

我要去旅行一年.

Wǒ yào qù lǚxíng yī nián.

famous sites

著名景点

zhùmíng jǐngdiǎn

luggage / baggage

行李

Xínglǐ

🏯 The Great Wall of China is a must-see destination. It extends over 13,000 miles (21,000 km)!

Great Wall of China

长城

Chángchéng

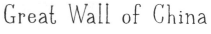

出发

departure

出发

chūfā

到达

arrival

到达

dàodá

33

Shopping

How much?

多少钱 / 几块钱
Duōshǎo qián / Jǐ kuài qián

shop / store
店
diàn

money
钱
qián

market / bazaar
市场
shìchǎng

yuan
元 / 人民币
yuán / rénmínbì

dollar
美元
měiyuán

customer / guest
客人
kèrén

supermarket
超市
chāo shì

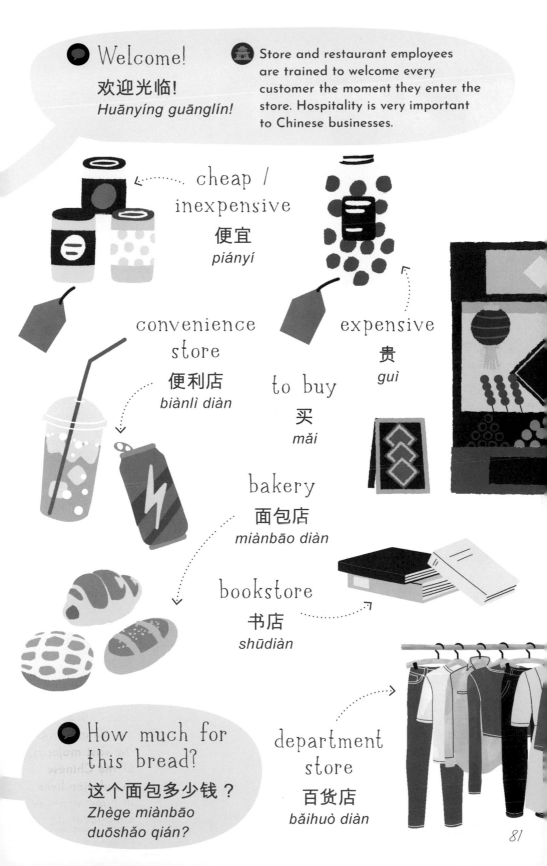

Welcome!
欢迎光临!
Huānyíng guānglín!

Store and restaurant employees are trained to welcome every customer the moment they enter the store. Hospitality is very important to Chinese businesses.

cheap / inexpensive
便宜
piányí

expensive
贵
guì

convenience store
便利店
biànlì diàn

to buy
买
mǎi

bakery
面包店
miànbāo diàn

bookstore
书店
shūdiàn

How much for this bread?
这个面包多少钱?
Zhège miànbāo duōshǎo qián?

department store
百货店
bǎihuò diàn

34

Home

to reside / to live
住
zhù

house
房子
fángzi

home
家
jiā

window
窗户
chuānghù

roof
屋顶
wūdǐng

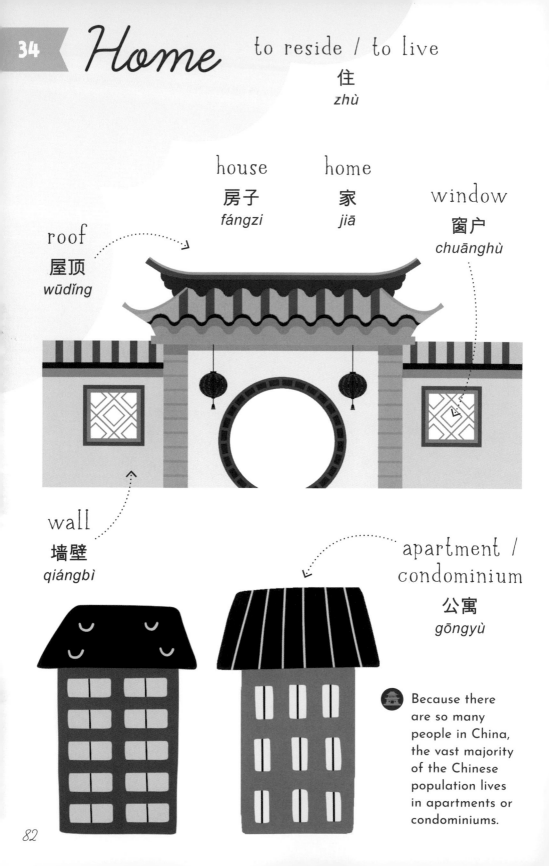

wall
墙壁
qiángbì

apartment /
condominium
公寓
gōngyù

Because there are so many people in China, the vast majority of the Chinese population lives in apartments or condominiums.

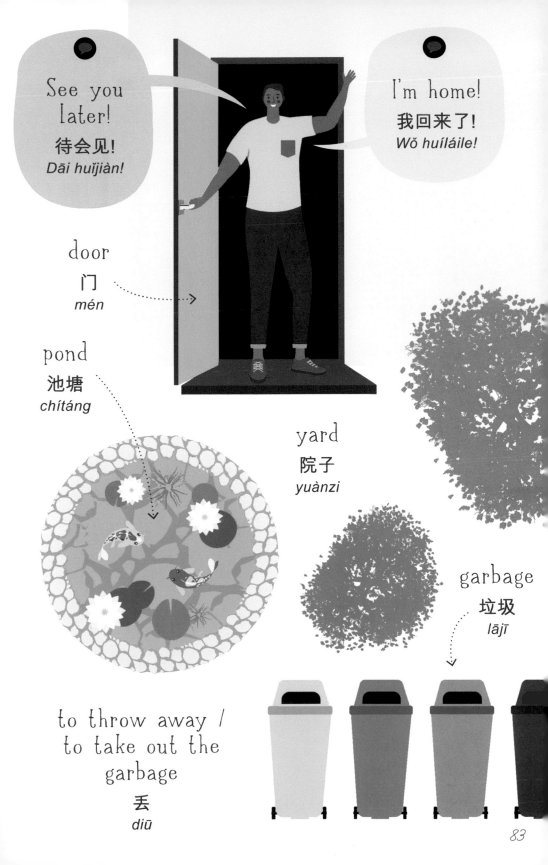

See you later!
待会见!
Dāi huǐjiàn!

I'm home!
我回来了!
Wǒ huíláile!

door
门
mén

pond
池塘
chítáng

yard
院子
yuànzi

garbage
垃圾
lājī

to throw away / to take out the garbage
丢
diū

35

Bedroom

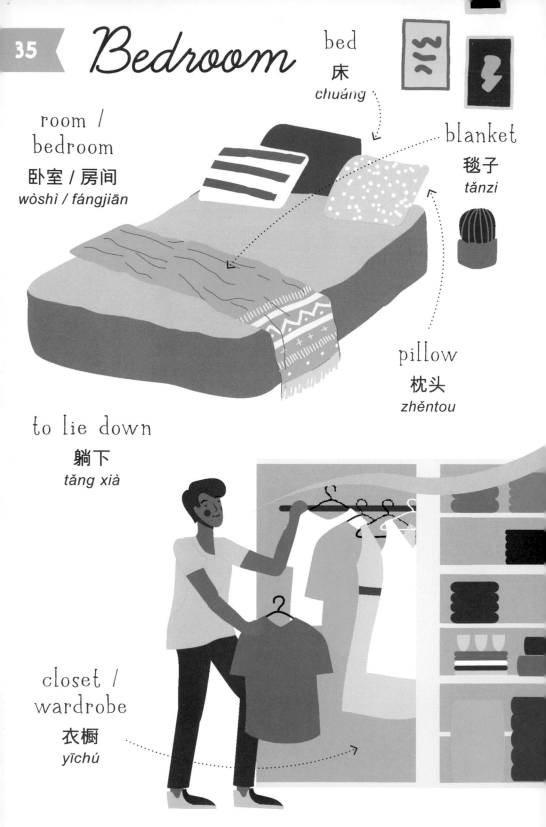

bed
床
chuáng

room /
bedroom
卧室 / 房间
wòshì / fángjiān

blanket
毯子
tǎnzi

pillow
枕头
zhěntou

to lie down
躺下
tǎng xià

closet /
wardrobe
衣橱
yīchú

Please organize your closet.
请整理你的衣橱.
Qǐng zhěnglǐ nǐ de yī chú.

bright
亮
liàng

dark
暗
àn

light
灯
dēng

to sleep
睡觉
shuìjiào

to awaken / to wake up
起床
qǐchuáng

light switch
电灯开关
diàndēng kāiguān

to turn on
开
kāi

mirror
镜子
jìngzi

to turn off
关
guān

toilet
马桶
mǎtǒng

bathroom
浴室
yùshì

to wash / to clean
洗
xǐ

shower
淋浴
línyù

to take
a bath
洗澡
xǐzǎo

bath
浴缸
yùgāng

to brush
teeth
刷牙
shuāyá

I need to wash my hands.
我需要洗手.
Wǒ xūyào xǐshǒu.

sink
洗手槽
xǐ shǒucáo

Kitchen

kitchen
厨房
chúfáng

microwave oven
微波炉
wēibōlú

refrigerator
冰箱
bīngxiāng

fire / flame
火
huǒ

stove
煤气炉
méiqì lú

oven
烤箱
kǎoxiāng

table
桌子
zhuōzi

chair
椅子
yǐzi

School

school
学校
xuéxiào

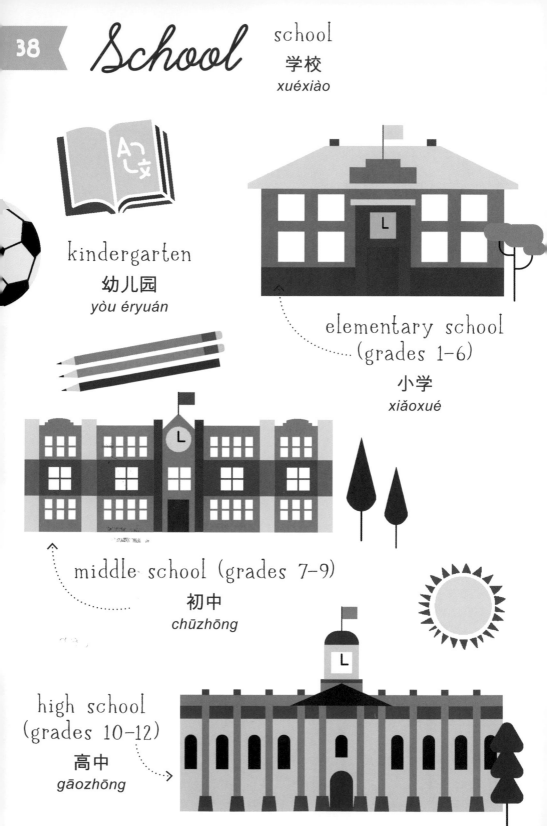

kindergarten
幼儿园
yòu éryuán

elementary school
(grades 1-6)
小学
xiǎoxué

middle school (grades 7-9)
初中
chūzhōng

high school
(grades 10-12)
高中
gāozhōng

uniform
制服
zhìfú

student
学生
xuéshēng

teacher /
instructor
老师
lǎoshī

university
大学
dàxué

university
cafeteria
食堂
shítáng

In Chinese universities, dorm students do not have kitchens to cook in, so they often go to the cafeteria for food. Luckily, school cafeterias are known for having really tasty (好吃 *hào chī*) and cheap (便宜 *piányí*) Chinese comfort foods!

university
student
大学生
dàxuéshēng

professor
教授
jiàoshòu

39

Classroom

classroom
教室
jiàoshì

to write
写
xiě

blackboard
黑板
hēibǎn

test / exam
考试
kǎoshì

诶 比 西 迪 伊 艾弗
A B C D E F

吉 艾尺 艾 杰 开 艾勒
G H I J K L

艾马 艾娜 哦 屁 吉吾 艾
M N O P Q R

艾丝 提 伊吾 维 豆贝尔维
S T U V W

艾克斯 吾艾 贼德
X Y Z

desk
课桌椅
kè zhuō yǐ

pencil
铅笔
qiānbǐ

pen
笔
bǐ

paper
纸
zhǐ

We must read our textbook.
我们必须阅读我们的课本.
Wǒmen bìxū yuèdú wǒmen de kèběn.

to read
阅读
yuèdú

book
书
shū

textbook
课本
kèběn

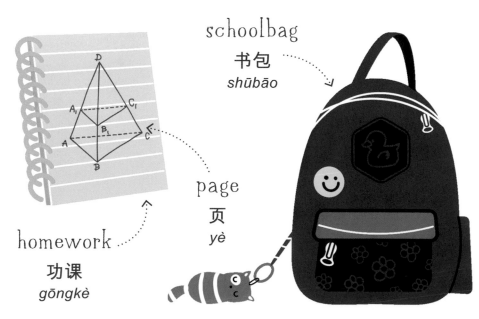

schoolbag
书包
shūbāo

homework
功课
gōngkè

page
页
yè

40

Subjects

education
教育
jiàoyù

school subject
课题 / 主题
kètí / zhǔtí

lesson / class
课
kè

language arts
语文
yǔwén

grammar
语法
yǔfǎ

Chinese language subject
中文课
zhōngwén kè

English language subject
英文课
yīngwén kè

mathemathics
数学
shùxué

MATHEMATICS

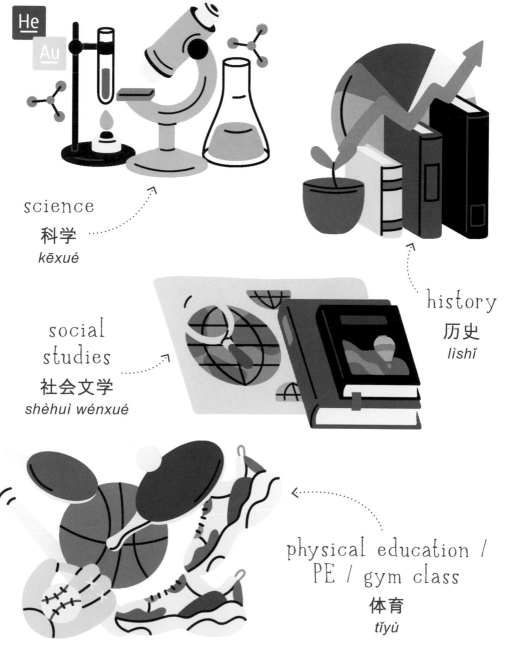

Chinese class is my favorite subject!
中文课是我最喜欢的课题!
Zhōngwén kè shì wǒ zuì xǐhuān de kètí!

science
科学
kēxué

history
历史
lìshǐ

social
studies
社会文学
shèhuì wénxué

physical education /
PE / gym class
体育
tǐyù

41

Health

health / healthy
健康
jiànkāng

injury / to
get injured
受伤
shòushāng

hurting /
pain
痛
tòng

energetic
充满精力
*chōngmǎn
jīnglì*

spirit /
mind /
energy
精神
jīngshén

to get sick
生病
shēngbìng

okay / safe
安全
ānquán

illness
疾病
jíbìng

bone
骨头
gǔtou

headache
头痛
tóutòng

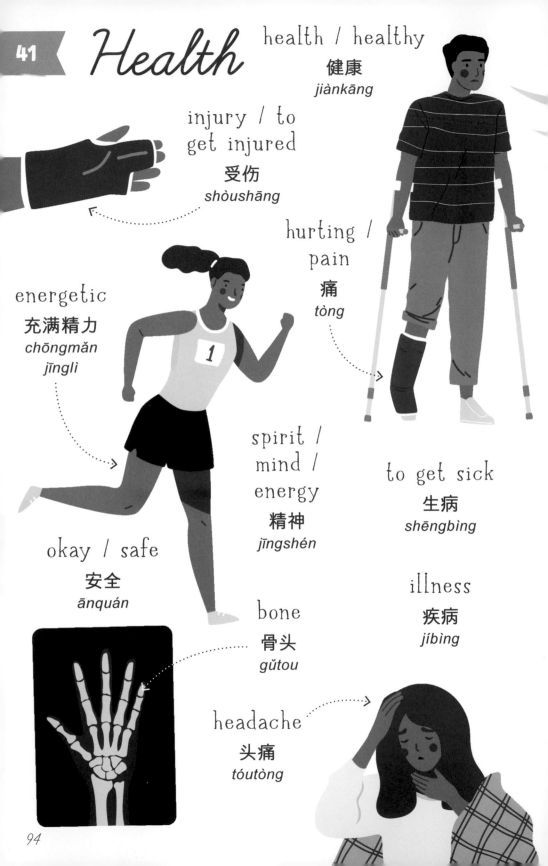

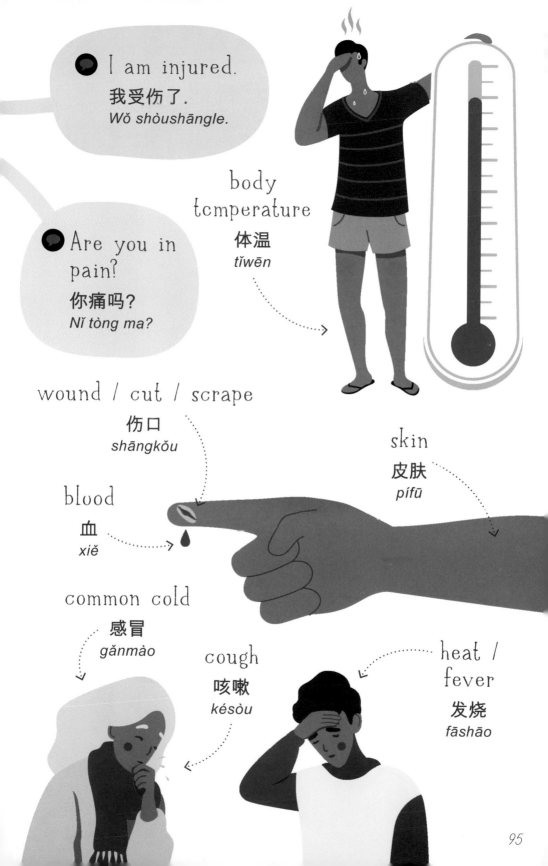

I am injured.
我受伤了.
Wǒ shòushāngle.

Are you in pain?
你痛吗?
Nǐ tòng ma?

body temperature
体温
tǐwēn

wound / cut / scrape
伤口
shāngkǒu

skin
皮肤
pífū

blood
血
xiě

common cold
感冒
gǎnmào

cough
咳嗽
késòu

heat / fever
发烧
fāshāo

42

Hobbies

hiking
爬山
páshān

hobby
爱好
àihào

to play sports (ball sports)
打球
dǎqiú

draw
画画
huàhuà

read
看书
kànshū

watch movies
看电影
kàn diànyǐng

knit
织毛线
zhī máoxiàn

game
游戏
yóuxì

play video games
打电动
dǎ diàndòng

China has the largest video gaming market in the world; almost half of the people play some sort of video game! And competitive gaming is incredibly popular, too.

music
音乐
yīnyuè

play piano
弹钢琴
tán gāngqín

gardening
园艺
yuányì

voice / sound
声音
shēngyīn

dance
跳舞
tiàowǔ

to sing
唱歌
chànggē

traditional Chinese opera
戏曲
xìqǔ

43

Sports

sports
运动
yùndòng

basketball
篮球
lánqiú

soccer
足球
zúqiú

athlete / player
运动员
yùndòngyuán

Basketball is by far the most popular sport in China.

badminton
羽毛球
yǔmáoqiú

team
球队
qiú duì

to win
赢
yíng

victory
胜利
shènglì

to lose
输
shū

defeat
打败
dǎbài

to exercise
锻炼
duànliàn

to walk
走路
zǒulù

to practice
练习
liànxí

to run
跑步
pǎobù

ping pong / table tennis
乒乓球
pīngpāng qiú

match / game
比赛
bǐsài

tennis
网球
wǎngqiú

volleyball
排球
páiqiú

swimming /
to swim
游泳
yóuyǒng

99

44

Martial Arts

martial arts
武术
wǔshù

Martial arts is a major part of Chinese culture and history. Dating all the way back to the Xia Dynasty (2070-1600 BCE), Chinese martial arts has grown to have hundreds of different styles today. The following are five of the most popular and well-known styles.

Shaolin Kung Fu
少林功夫
shàolín gōngfū

Developed by monks of the Shaolin Temple in the Henan province, Shaolin Kung Fu is one of the most popular styles of martial arts. Today, there are hundreds of sub-styles of Shaolin Kung Fu. This style of Kung Fu uses quick, forceful movements and weapons, including swords, spears, and most famously, staffs.

Tai Chi
太极拳
tàijíquán

Tai Chi, which is now mostly practiced as a meditative exercise, was founded on the idea of meeting brute force with softness. Its roots come from the ancient Taoist philosophies of balance. This style focuses on self-defense movements that redirect the oncoming force of opponents, causing them to exhaust themselves.

Wing Chun
咏春
yǒngchūn

Wing Chun, like Tai Chi, is a style that focuses on technique over strength. It is a style of fighting that requires the user to remain relaxed while fighting in order to achieve a softness or flexibility that resembles bamboo. Wing Chun was famously learned and practiced by martial arts master Bruce Lee.

Bajiquan
八极拳
bājíquán

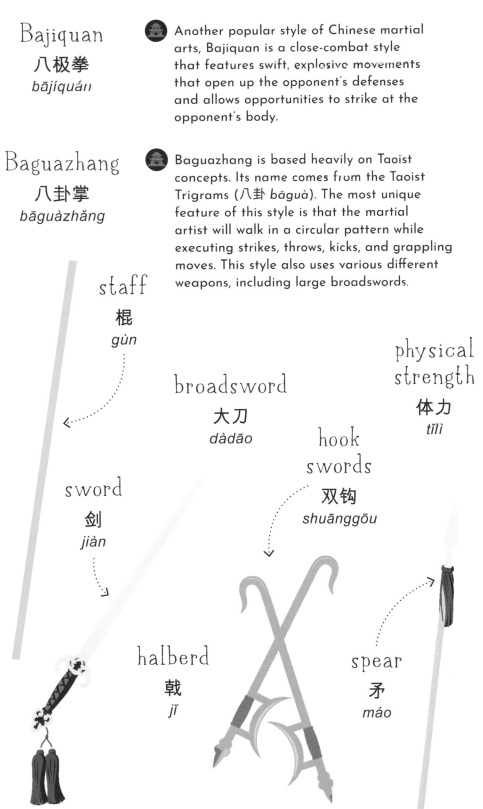

Another popular style of Chinese martial arts, Bajiquan is a close-combat style that features swift, explosive movements that open up the opponent's defenses and allows opportunities to strike at the opponent's body.

Baguazhang
八卦掌
bāguàzhǎng

Baguazhang is based heavily on Taoist concepts. Its name comes from the Taoist Trigrams (八卦 *bāguà*). The most unique feature of this style is that the martial artist will walk in a circular pattern while executing strikes, throws, kicks, and grappling moves. This style also uses various different weapons, including large broadswords.

staff
棍
gùn

physical
strength
体力
tǐlì

broadsword
大刀
dàdāo

hook
swords
双钩
shuānggōu

sword
剑
jiàn

halberd
戟
jǐ

spear
矛
máo

45

Festivals

festival

节日

jiérì

Chinese New Year is one of the most important Chinese festivals and dates back over 4,000 years. The celebration begins on the first day of the lunar calendar and lasts for two weeks. During this festival, it is customary to wear the color red, hang red banners and decorations, and set off Chinese firecrackers.

fireworks

烟火 / 烟花

yānhuǒ / yānhuā

Chinese firecrackers

鞭炮

biānpào

Chinese New Year (Spring Festival)

新年 (春节)

Xīnnián (Chūnjié)

ancestral
shrine
祠堂
cítáng

Tomb Sweeping
Day
清明节
Qīngmíng jié

incense
香
xiāng

offerings
供品
gòngpǐn

temple
庙
miào

During Tomb Sweeping
Day and Hungry Ghost
Festival, everyone goes to
their ancestral shrines to
pay respect, burn incense,
and bring food and drink
offerings to their ancestors.

Hungry Ghost
Festival
中元节
Zhōng yuán jié

celebrate
庆祝
qìngzhù

Mid-Autumn Festival
中秋节
Zhōngqiū jié

National Day
国庆节
Guóqìngjié

National Day commemorates October 1, 1949, the day the People's Republic of China was founded.

Dragon Boat Festival
端午节
Duānwǔ jié

sticky rice dumplings (zongzi)
粽子
zòngzi

These dumplings are a delicious traditional Chinese dish made from glutinous rice stuffed with different fillings and wrapped in bamboo leaves. Zongzi is eaten every year during Dragon Boat Festival (端午节).

Lantern Festival
元宵节
yuánxiāo jié

lantern
灯笼
dēnglóng

Winter
Solstice
Festival
冬至
Dōngzhì

Tang yuan is a traditional Chinese dish made from rice flour and is eaten during many Chinese festivals, including *Yuánxiāo jié* (元宵节) and *Dōngzhì* (冬至). "Tang yuan" is the term used in southern China; in northern China, it's called "yuan xiao."

tang yuan
汤圆
tāngyuán

yuan xiao
元宵
yuánxiāo

American Holidays

holiday
节日
jiérì

Easter
复活节
Fùhuó jié

Halloween
万圣节
Wànshèngjié

Thanksgiving
感恩节
Gǎn'ēn jié

Mother's Day
母亲节
Mǔqīn jié

Father's Day
父亲节
Fùqīn jié

Independence Day
独立日
Dúlì rì

Christmas
圣诞节
Shèngdàn jié

Valentine's Day
情人节
Qíngrén jié

New Year's Day
元旦
Yuándàn

Communication

to speak /
to talk
说话
shuōhuà

to say
说
shuō

cell phone
手机
shǒujī

💡 Literally translates to "hand machine"

"Hello?"
喂?
Wéi?

make a phone call
打电话
dǎ diànhuà

telephone
电话
diànhuà

radio
收音机
shōuyīnjī

TV / television
电视
diànshì

internet
互联网
hùliánwǎng

computer
电脑
diànnǎo

post office
邮局
yóujú

mailbox
邮箱
yóuxiāng

postcard
明信片
míngxìnpiàn

mail
邮件
yóujiàn

letter
信
xìn

48

Fairy Tales

story / tale
故事
gùshì

goblin / monster
妖怪
yāoguài

demon
恶魔
èmó

ghost story
鬼故事
guǐ gùshì

prince
王子
Wángzǐ

princess
公主
Gōngzhǔ

king
国王
Guówáng

queen
王后
Wánghòu

emperor
皇帝
huángdì

empress
皇后
huánghòu

castle
城堡
chéngbǎo

once upon
a time
从前
cóngqián

legend / folktale
传说
chuánshuō

mythology
神话
shénhuà

Journey to
the West
西游记
Xīyóu jì

"Journey to the West" is China's most famous mythological story. It features the Monkey King, who can be found in many different forms of pop culture.

dragon
龙
lóng

49

Meals

meal	food	to eat
餐	食物	吃
cān	shíwù	chī

"Come eat."
吃饭.
Chī fàn.

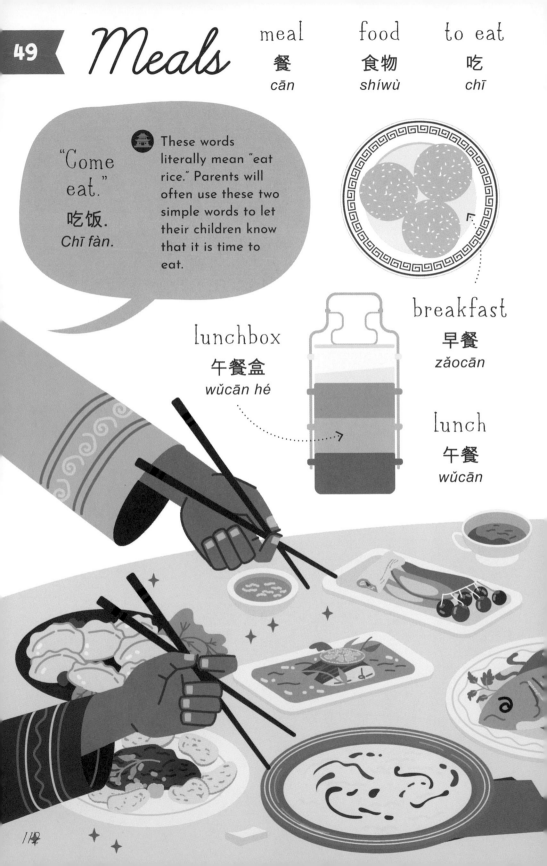

These words literally mean "eat rice." Parents will often use these two simple words to let their children know that it is time to eat.

breakfast
早餐
zǎocān

lunchbox
午餐盒
wǔcān hé

lunch
午餐
wǔcān

rice (uncooked)

米
mǐ

cooked rice / meal (commonly used)

饭
fàn

midnight snack

夜宵
yè xiāo

dinner

晚餐
wǎncān

50

Drink

to drink
喝
hē

drink / beverage
饮料
yǐnliào

ice water
冰水
bīng shuǐ

boba / pearl milk tea
珍珠奶茶
zhēnzhū nǎichá

hot water
热水
rè shuǐ

tea
茶
chá

green tea
绿茶
lǜchá

black tea
红茶
hóngchá

coffee
咖啡
kāfēi

vending
machine
自动售货机
zìdòng shòu huòjī

milk
牛奶
niúnǎi

soda
汽水
qìshuǐ

fruit juice
果汁
guǒzhī

115

Fruits

fruit
水果
shuǐguǒ

apple
苹果
píngguǒ

dragon
fruit
火龙果
huǒlóng guǒ

pear
梨
lí

peach
桃子
táozi

mandarin
orange
桔子
júzi

kiwi
猕猴桃
míhóutáo

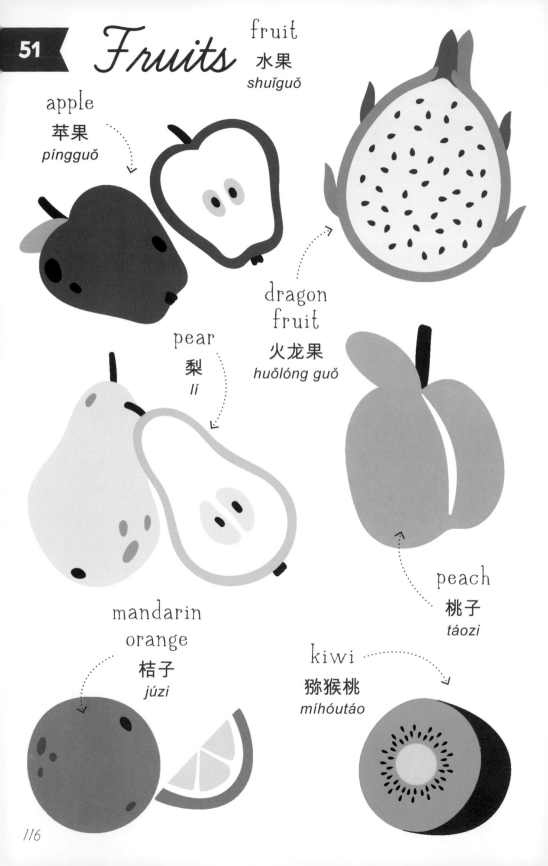

strawberry
草莓
cǎoméi

grape
葡萄
pútáo

lychee
荔枝
lìzhī

melon
瓜
guā

mango
芒果
mángguǒ

watermelon
西瓜
xīguā

papaya
木瓜
mùguā

117

52

Vegetables

vegetable
蔬菜
shūcài

carrot
胡萝卜
húluóbo

tomato
西红柿 / 番茄
xīhóngshì / fānqié

eggplant
茄子
qiézi

green onion /
scallion
葱
cōng

onion
洋葱
yángcōng

potato
土豆
tǔdòu

garlic
大蒜
dàsuàn

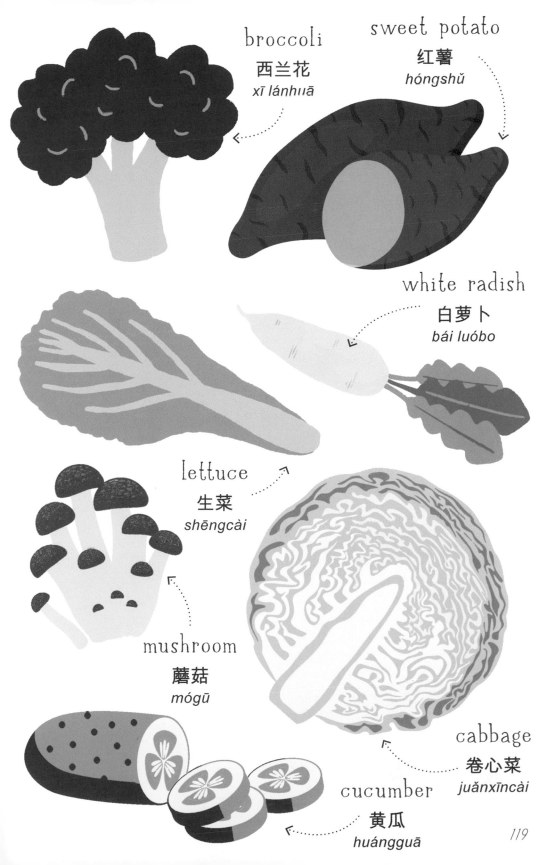

broccoli
西兰花
xī lánhuā

sweet potato
红薯
hóngshǔ

white radish
白萝卜
bái luóbo

lettuce
生菜
shēngcài

mushroom
蘑菇
mógū

cabbage
卷心菜
juǎnxīncài

cucumber
黄瓜
huángguā

53

Meat, Dairy, and Eggs

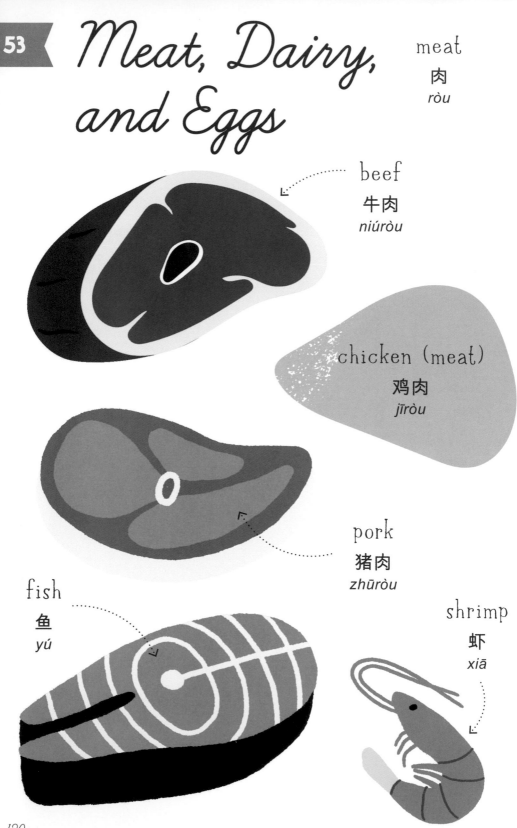

meat
肉
ròu

beef
牛肉
niúròu

chicken (meat)
鸡肉
jīròu

pork
猪肉
zhūròu

fish
鱼
yú

shrimp
虾
xiā

egg
蛋
dàn

shellfish
贝类
bèi lèi

tofu
豆腐
dòufu

cheese
芝士
zhīshì

butter
黄油
huángyóu

yogurt
酸奶
suānnǎi

Cooking

to cook
煮饭 / 煮菜
zhǔ fàn / zhǔ cài

ingredients
食材
shícái

soy sauce
酱油
jiàngyóu

to bake / to grill
烤
kǎo

chef
厨师
chúshī

to stir-fry
炒
chǎo

to steam
蒸
zhēng

chopsticks
筷子
kuàizi

bowl
碗
wǎn

plate
盘子
pánzi

cup / glass
杯子
bēizi

sugar
糖
táng

knife
刀
dāo

fork
叉子
chāzi

salt
盐
yán

spoon
勺子
sháozi

pepper
胡椒
hújiāo

recipe
食谱
shípǔ

flavor / taste
味道
wèidào

kitchen knife
菜刀
càidāo

pot / saucepan
锅
guō

to cut
切
qiē

frying pan / skillet
平底锅
píngdǐ guō

cutting board
切菜板
qiē cài bǎn

55

Cuisine

delicious
好吃
hǎo chī

sweet
甜
tián

savory / salty
咸
xián

restaurant
餐厅
cāntīng

In China, it is not customary to leave a tip when eating out at a restaurant. In fact, it can sometimes be considered rude or disrespectful!

fried squid
炸鱿鱼
zhà yóuyú

fried rice
炒饭
chǎofàn

street kebabs
烤肉串
kǎoròu chuàn

Dumplings are a traditional dish of meat and veggies wrapped into flour dough and steamed or boiled to perfection. Because dumplings resemble the shape of ancient Chinese gold ingots, they are often eaten during the Chinese New Year celebrations to bring wealth and good fortune.

dumplings
水饺
shuǐjiǎo

The iconic roast duck can be found in window displays from Beijing to Chinatowns all over the world. Paired with sweet sauce, cucumber sticks, and green onions, this delicious treat is a must-have!

roast duck
烤鸭
kǎoyā

hot pot
火锅
huǒguō

Not only is hot pot incredibly delicious, it is also very easy to make! With a boiling pot of yummy broth, all you have to do is add raw meat and veggies, let them cook thoroughly, and serve with your favorite sauce. It's a diverse meal with many different flavors!

Hand-pulled noodles are the origin of Japanese ramen and a delicious Chinese comfort food. Every region in China has their own special take.

hand-pulled noodles
拉面
lāmiàn

mapo tofu

Mapo tofu is a famous, spicy dish originating from the Sichuan province. On a scale of 1-10, how spicy can you handle?

麻婆豆腐
má pó dòufu

Fried eggs with tomatoes is an easy dish that is favored by the elderly and children because of its sweet and sour flavors.

fried eggs with tomatoes
西红柿炒鸡蛋
xīhóngshì chǎo jīdàn

Chinese buns
包子
bāozi

These simple buns originated in northern China and come with different fillings and flavors. While they're most commonly filled with meat and veggies, they can also be made sweet with black-sesame or taro paste.

125

56

Numbers

digit / numeral
数字
shùzì

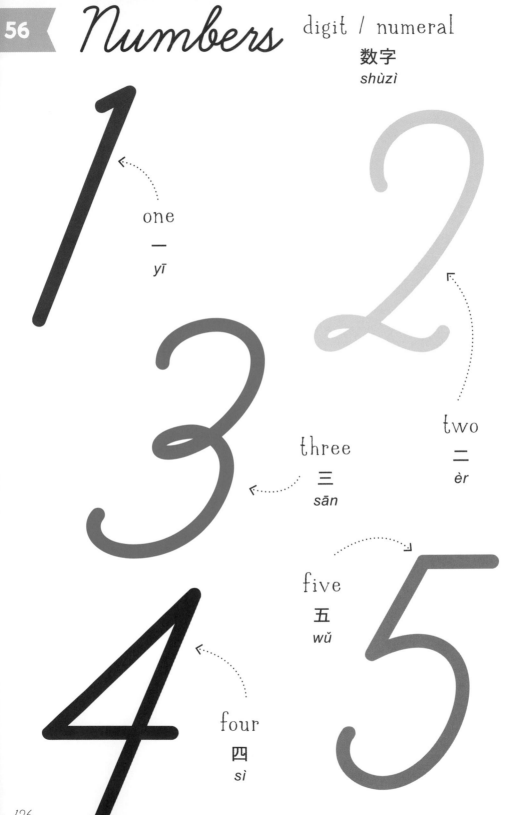

one
一
yī

two
二
èr

three
三
sān

four
四
sì

five
五
wǔ

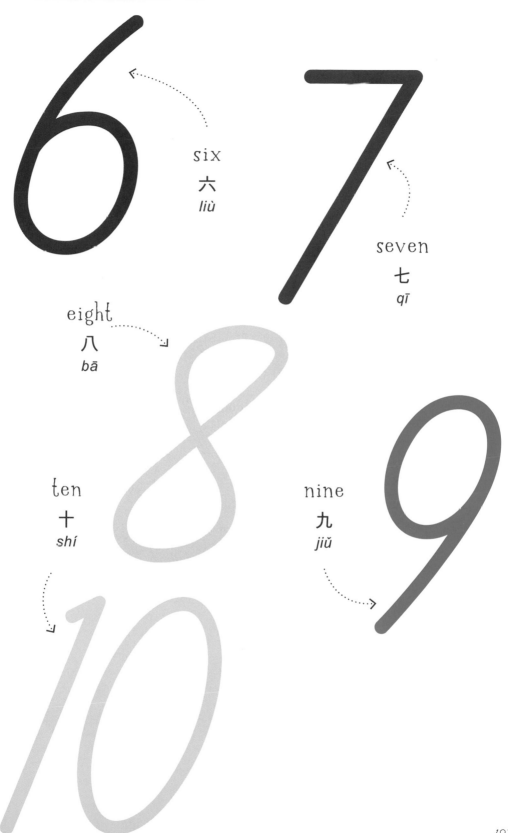

6 six
六
liù

7 seven
七
qī

eight
八
bā
8

nine
九
jiǔ
9

ten
十
shí
10

57

Making Numbers

💡 Counting in Chinese is easy once you get the hang of it! All you have to do is memorize the first ten numbers and some counters for the bigger numbers. The counters we will be learning in this book (which are listed in the next section) go from tens to hundreds to thousands to tens of thousands.

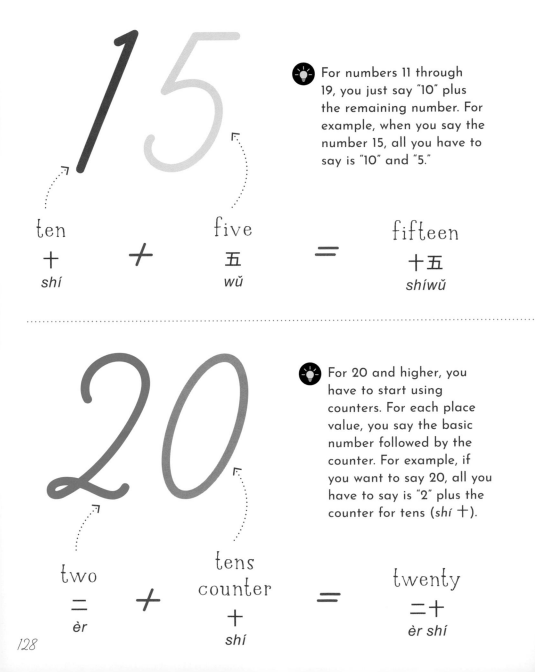

💡 For numbers 11 through 19, you just say "10" plus the remaining number. For example, when you say the number 15, all you have to say is "10" and "5."

ten		five		fifteen
十	+	五	=	十五
shí		*wǔ*		*shíwǔ*

💡 For 20 and higher, you have to start using counters. For each place value, you say the basic number followed by the counter. For example, if you want to say 20, all you have to say is "2" plus the counter for tens (*shí* 十).

two		tens counter		twenty
二	+	十	=	二十
èr		*shí*		*èr shí*

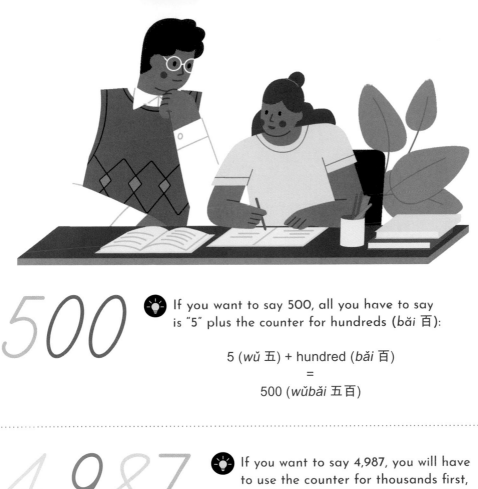

500

If you want to say 500, all you have to say is "5" plus the counter for hundreds (*bǎi* 百):

5 (*wǔ* 五) + hundred (*bǎi* 百)
=
500 (*wǔbǎi* 五百)

4,987

If you want to say 4,987, you will have to use the counter for thousands first, then hundreds second, then tens third, and finally the basic number.

4,000 (*sìqiān* 四千) + 900 (*jiǔbǎi* 九百) + 80 (*bāshí* 八十) + 7 (*qī* 七)
=
4,987 (*sìqiān jiǔbǎi bāshí qī* 四千九百八十七)

34,179

If you want to say 34,179, all you have to do is construct the pieces together in order, using the highest number and counter to the lowest number and counter.

30,000 (*sānwàn* 三万) + 4,000 (*sìqiān* 四千) + 100 (*yībǎi* 一百) + 70 (*qīshí* 七十) + 9 (*jiǔ* 九)

= 34,179 (*sānwàn sìqiān yībǎi qīshí jiǔ* 三万四千一百七十九)

58

Bigger Numbers

	Counter for 10s (*shí* 十)		
11	eleven	十一	*shí yī*
12	twelve	十二	*shí èr*
13	thirteen	十三	*shí sān*
14	fourteen	十四	*shí sì*
15	fifteen	十五	*shí wǔ*
16	sixteen	十六	*shí liù*
17	seventeen	十七	*shí qī*
18	eighteen	十八	*shí bā*
19	nineteen	十九	*shí jiǔ*
20	twenty	二十	*èr shí*
30	thirty	三十	*sān shí*
40	forty	四十	*sì shí*
50	fifty	五十	*wǔ shí*
60	sixty	六十	*liù shí*
70	seventy	七十	*qī shí*
80	eighty	八十	*bā shí*
90	ninety	九十	*jiǔ shí*
	Counter for 100s (*bǎi* 百)		
100	one hundred	一百	*yī bǎi*
200	two hundred	两百	*liǎng bǎi*
300	three hundred	三百	*sān bǎi*
400	four hundred	四百	*sì bǎi*
500	five hundred	五百	*wǔ bǎi*

600	six hundred	六百	*liù bǎi*
700	seven hundred	七百	*qī bǎi*
800	eight hundred	八百	*bā bǎi*
900	nine hundred	九百	*jiǔ bǎi*

Counter for 1,000s (*qiān* 千)

1,000	one thousand	一千	*yī qiān*
2,000	two thousand	两千	*liǎng qiān*
3,000	three thousand	三千	*sān qiān*
4,000	four thousand	四千	*sì qiān*
5,000	five thousand	五千	*wǔ qiān*
6,000	six thousand	六千	*liù qiān*
7,000	seven thousand	七千	*qī qiān*
8,000	eight thousand	八千	*bā qiān*
9,000	nine thousand	九千	*jiǔ qiān*

Counter for 10,000s (*yī wàn* 一万)

10,000	ten thousand	一万	*yī wàn*
20,000	twenty thousand	两万	*liǎng wàn*
30,000	thirty thousand	三万	*sān wàn*
40,000	forty thousand	四万	*sì wàn*
50,000	fifty thousand	五万	*wǔ wàn*
60,000	sixty thousand	六万	*liù wàn*
70,000	seventy thousand	七万	*qī wàn*
80,000	eighty thousand	八万	*bā wàn*
90,000	ninety thousand	九万	*jiǔ wàn*

59

Measure Words

When saying a specific number of things, Mandarin Chinese uses special measure words along with the noun being counted. It's similar to how one might say "two cups of flour" instead of "two flours" in English, only it applies to everything. In Chinese, there are over 100 different measure words, but we will learn only a few common ones here.

1 one (object)
一个
yī gè

2 two (objects)
两个
liǎng gè

3 three (objects)
三个
sān gè

4 four (objects)
四个
sì gè

5 five (objects)
五个
wǔ gè

6 six (objects)
六个
liù gè

7 seven (objects)
七个
qī gè

8 eight (objects)
八个
bā gè

9 nine (objects)
九个
jiǔ gè

10 ten (objects)
十个
shí gè

YEARS OLD

years
old
measure
word

岁
suì

🗨 Happy
birthday!
生日快乐!
Shēngrì kuàilè!

---

1 one year old
一岁
yī suì

2 two years old
两岁
liǎng suì

3 three years old
三岁
sān suì

4 four years old
四岁
sì suì

5 five years old
五岁
wǔ suì

6 six years old
六岁
liù suì

7 seven years old
七岁
qī suì

8 eight years old
八岁
bā suì

9 nine years old
九岁
jiǔ suì

10 ten years old
十岁
shí suì

measure word for people
个人 / 位
gè rén / wèi (polite)

PEOPLE

1 one person / alone
一个人 / 一位
yī gè rén / yī wèi

2 two people
两个人 / 两位
liǎng gè rén / liǎng wèi

3 three people
三个人 / 三位
sān gè rén / sān wèi

4 four people
四个人 / 四位
sì gè rén / sì wèi

5 five people
五个人 / 五位
wǔ gè rén / wǔ wèi

6 six people
六个人 / 六位
liù gè rén / liù wèi

7 seven people
七个人 / 七位
qī gè rén / qī wèi

8 eight people
八个人 / 八位
bā gè rén / bā wèi

9 nine people
九个人 / 九位
jiǔ gè rén / jiǔ wèi

10 ten people
十个人 / 十位
shí gè rén / shí wèi

OTHER MEASURE WORDS

measure word for money
元 / 块
yuán / kuài

generic measure word for small animals
只
zhī

Used for birds, dogs, pigs, etc.

measure word for things with long, narrow shapes
条
tiáo

Used for fish, snakes, ropes, roads, pants, etc.

measure word for flat objects
张
zhāng

Used for paper, tickets, or stamps.

measure word for days
天
tiān

measure word for vehicles with wheels
辆
liàng

Used for cars, buses, bikes, scooters, etc.

135

Word Index

ABOUT THE AUTHOR

Timothy Tsai grew up in Provo, Utah. Born as a Chinese American and raised by immigrant parents, Tim learned English at school while learning Chinese at home. Tim was taught by his parents to diligently preserve his family's Chinese heritage. He has also been fortunate enough to visit family back in China on several occasions to learn more about his ancestors and their traditions, values, and culture.

Tim has always had a fascination with different languages. Having taken Spanish classes, French classes, Japanese classes, and even some Chinese classes, he has had plenty of experiences as a novice language learner and understands the time and effort it takes to master a language.

Tim currently resides in Orem, Utah, with his wife and is obtaining a master's degree to become a marriage and family therapist. When he is not working or studying, he enjoys playing video games, playing basketball, reading books, watching anime, and spending quality time with his wife, family, and friends.

ABOUT BUSHEL & PECK BOOKS

Bushel & Peck Books is a children's publishing house with a special mission. Through our Book-for-Book Promise™, we donate one book to kids in need for every book we sell. Our beautiful books are given to kids through schools, libraries, local neighborhoods, shelters, nonprofits, and also to many selfless organizations that are working hard to make a difference. So thank you for purchasing this book! Because of you, another book will make its way into the hands of a child who needs it most.

NOMINATE A SCHOOL OR ORGANIZATION TO RECEIVE FREE BOOKS

Do you know a school, library, or organization that could use some free books for their kids? We'd love to help! Please fill out the nomination form on our website, and we'll do everything we can to make something happen.

www.bushelandpeckbooks.com/pages/
nominate-a-school-or-organization

If you liked this book, please leave a review online at your favorite retailer. Honest reviews spread the word about Bushel & Peck—and help us make better books, too!